For Reference

Not to be taken from this room

Date: 10/17/11

J REF 590 HAM
Hammond, Paula.
Atlas of the world's strangest
animals /

W9-AOJ-681

PALM BEACH COUNTY
LIBRARY SYSTEM
3650 SUMMIT BLVD.
WEST PALM BEACH, FL 33406

ATLAS OF THE WORLD'S
STRANGEST
ANIMALS

ATLAS OF THE WORLD'S
STRANGEST
ANIMALS

PAULA HAMMOND

Marshall Cavendish
Reference

NEW YORK

This edition first published in 2011 in the United States of America by Marshall Cavendish.

Copyright © 2011 Amber Books Ltd

Published by Marshall Cavendish Reference
An imprint of Marshall Cavendish Corporation

All rights reserved.

No part of this publication may be reproduced, stored in a retrieval system or transmitted, in any form or by any means, electronic, mechanical, photocopying, recording, or otherwise, without the prior permission of the copyright owner. Request for permission should be addressed to the Publisher, Marshall Cavendish Corporation, 99 White Plains Road, Tarrytown, NY 10591. Tel: (914) 332-8888, fax: (914) 332-1888.

Website: www.marshallcavendish.us

This publication represents the opinions and views of the authors based on personal experience, knowledge, and research. The information in this book serves as a general guide only. The author and publisher have used their best efforts in preparing this book and disclaim liability rising directly and indirectly from the use and application of this book.

Other Marshall Cavendish Offices:
Marshall Cavendish International (Asia) Private Limited, 1 New Industrial Road, Singapore 536196 • Marshall Cavendish International (Thailand) Co Ltd. 253 Asoke, 12th Flr, Sukhumvit 21 Road, Klongtoey Nua, Wattana, Bangkok 10110, Thailand • Marshall Cavendish (Malaysia) Sdn Bhd, Times Subang, Lot 46, Subang Hi-Tech Industrial Park, Batu Tiga, 40000 Shah Alam, Selangor Darul Ehsan, Malaysia

Marshall Cavendish is a trademark of Times Publishing Limited

All websites were available and accurate when this book was sent to press.

Library of Congress Cataloging-in-Publication Data

Hammond, Paula.
    Atlas of the world's strangest animals / Paula Hammond.
      p. cm.
    Includes bibliographical references and index.
    ISBN 978-0-7614-7940-6 (alk. paper)
    1. Animals–Juvenile literature. 2. Animals–Geographical distribution–Juvenile literature. I. Title.
    QL49.H284 2010
    590–dc22
                                    2010014802

Printed in China

14 13 12 11 10   1 2 3 4 5

Editorial and design by
Amber Books Ltd
Bradley's Close
74–77 White Lion Street
London N1 9PF
United Kingdom
www.amberbooks.co.uk

Project editor: Sarah Uttridge
Editorial Assistant: Kieron Connolly
Designer: Itonic Design Ltd

Artwork credits: All © International Masters Publishing Ltd
Photo credits: **Dreamstime:** 23 (Heinz Effner), 37 (Siloto), 44 (Anthony Hall), 75 (Ongchangwei), 117 (Artur Tomasz Komorowski), 191 (Steffen Foerster), 199 (Maya Paulin), 202 (John Abramo); **FLPA:** 10 (ZSSD/Minden Pictures), 30 (Ron Austing), 41 (Stephen Belcher/Minden Pictures), 67 (Foto Natura Stock), 91 (Scott Linstead/Minden Pictures), 108 (Scott Linstead/Minden Pictures), 138 (Heidi & Hans-Juergen Koch/Minden Pictures), 154 (Thomas Marent/Minden Pictures), 172 (Matt Cole), 185 (Gerard Lacz), 206 (Flip Nicklin/Minden Pictures), 211 (Norbert Wu/Minden Pictures); Fotolia: 60 (Herbert Kratky), 70 (Seraphic 06); **iStockphoto:** 57 (Susan Stewart), 135 (Marshall Bruce), 218 (Alex Koen); **Photos.com:** 15, 27, 83, 96, 194; **Stock.Xchang:** 86 (David Hewitt), 214 (Obe Nix); **Webshots:** 112 (Addan 104); **Wikipedia Creative Commons Licence:** 78 (Dacelo Novaguineae), 126 (Mila Zinkova), 143 (Malene Thyssen)

Contents

Introduction

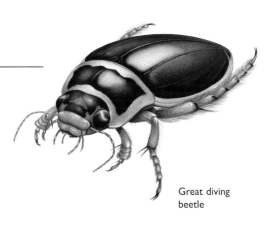

Great diving beetle

According to a study in 2007, 1,263,186 animal species have so far been been named and scientifically described. This includes 950,000 species of insects, 9956 birds, 8240 reptiles, 6199 amphibians and 5416 mammals. When we consider that there are still parts of the world that are so inhospitable no human has ever set foot there, then it's possible we may never know for sure just how many species we really share our planet with. However, what is certain is that many of the animals we are familiar with are truly remarkable. If we were to flick through this list of 1,263,186 species then, within it, we would find some of nature's greatest curiosities: mammals that can fly and birds that can't; frogs as small as fingernails and birds as big as horses. Here, we'd discover walking fish, brainless jellies, cannibals and camouflage experts.

Tarsier

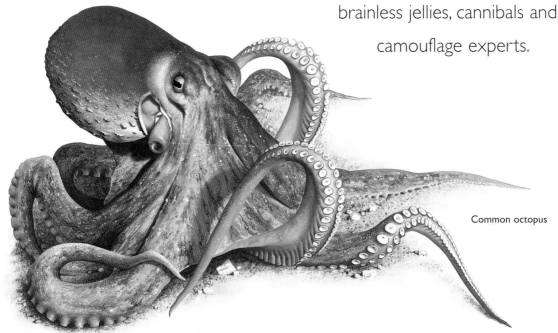

Common octopus

Three-toed sloth

Sugar glider

Life, it seems, comes in all shapes and sizes – many of them very strange indeed. Who, for instance, could have invented a fish with its own, in-built fishing rod; a poisonous mammal that lays eggs; or brightly coloured reef-dwellers that run their own, highly successful cleaning 'service'? In this book you'll find 50 of these seriously strange creatures including some, perhaps, that we're so well acquainted with, at first glance, they may seem quite mundane. If only we were able to fully explore the deepest oceans, driest deserts and highest mountain tops, then who knows what other marvels we might add to this list of wonders?

Mantis

Naked mole rat

EUROPE

MEDITERRANEAN SEA

Atlas Mountains

Sahara

Nile

Nubian
Desert

ARABIAN
SEA

SOUTH ATLANTIC

OCEAN

Congo
Basin

Lake
Victoria

AFRICA

MADAGASCAR

INDIAN

OCEAN

Namib Desert

Kalahari
Desert

Cape of Good Hope

Africa

From dew-drenched forests to parched deserts, from glorious grasslands to sun-baked beaches, Africa is a continent that both stimulates and surprises.

This vast landmass, spread across 300,330,000 square kilometres (11,600 square miles), is the world's second-largest continent, encompassing more than 50 nations and a billion people. In the north of this tear-shaped land is the great Sahara Desert, which sprawls, untamed, across an area larger than the United States of America. On the edge of this sea of sand, the desert starts to disappear, giving birth to swathes of scrubby grassland known as savannah. These are regions that depend on one season of the year for most of their rainfall, and many animals roam across these regions in pursuit of the rains. In fact, the Serengeti savannah plays host each year to the largest, longest overland migration in the world.

In central Africa, nestled in the Congo Basin, is the continent's great rainforest. This beautiful region is the second-largest rainforest on Earth. It's an area of dense, steamy jungle, which contains around 70 per cent of all of Africa's plant life and an estimated 10,000 animal species – many found nowhere else.

Thanks to such a rich variety of 'ecosystems', the African continent supports a bewildering array of weird and wonderful wildlife. It's here that you'll find many of the world's biggest, fastest and most dangerous species. It's also home to some of our planet's animal 'superstars' – the elephants, lions and zebras that appear so often on our television screens. But there's more to this amazing land than killer cats and wild game. In this section, you'll read about some of Africa's more curious inhabitants – rodents that behave like insects, 'living fossils' and some genuinely strange record-breakers!

Aardvark

Aardvarks are surely Africa's most curious-looking mammals. With their almost hairless bodies, rabbit-like ears, a toothless snout and snakelike tongue, these 'earth pigs' are so odd that scientists still struggle to classify them. With no known relatives they have been described as 'living fossils'.

Key Facts	ORDER *Tubulidentata* / FAMILY *Orycteropodidae* / GENUS & SPECIES *Orycteropus afer*
Weight	49.9–81.6kg (110–180lb)
Length	Up to 1.8m (6ft) including tail
Sexual maturity	2 years
Breeding season	May–June near equator; October–November southern Africa
Number of young	Number of young: 1
Gestation period	7 months
Breeding interval	Yearly
Typical diet	Typical diet: Termites and other insects
Lifespan	Up to 23 years in captivity

Teeth

Aardvarks have no front teeth. Instead, they rely on strong 'cheek teeth' at the back of the mouth to grind up food.

Claws

Partially webbed second and third toes and a set of strong, sharp, hooflike claws make aardvarks superb tunnellers and diggers.

Ears

Being night-time specialists means that aardvarks must rely, primarily, on their senses of smell and hearing to track down termites.

'Aardvark' is famously one of the first words you'll find in an English language dictionary. The name comes from Dutch Afrikaans and means 'earth pig', which is exactly what European settlers thought these strange mammals looked like. However, although these shy and solitary creatures do have piglike bodies, they're no relation. In fact, genetically speaking, aardvarks are a puzzle.

When classifying living things, scientists begin by looking for similarities between known species. But can you think of any other burrowing, nocturnal mammal that has a powerful tail, rabbit-like ears, webbed toes, claws resembling hooves and a long sticky tongue? It's a problem that has stumped scientists for decades.

Initially, the solution was to choose a 'best fit' by placing the aardvark in the same order as armadillos and sloths *(Edentata)*. Later, a new order was created especially for the aardvark – *Tubulidentata*. Edentata means 'toothless ones' and armadillos and sloths both lack front, incisor teeth. Adult aardvarks have no front teeth either, but they do possess extremely odd 'cheek teeth' at the back of their jaws. In place of the usual 'pulp' in the centre of each tooth are fine tubes bound together by a hard substance called cementum. Hence the name *'Tubulidentata'*, meaning tube-toothed.

To date, the aardvark is the only known member of the order *'Tubulidentata'* and the situation is likely to remain that way. Although a few fossilized remains have been found, they provide no clues to the aardvarks' ancestry or their relationship to other species. These curious beasts

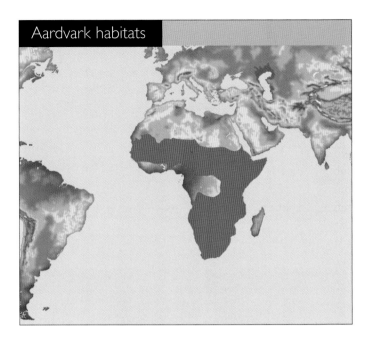

Aardvark habitats

seem to be living fossils. They may have been very successful as a species, but they're an evolutionary dead end. They have distant relatives today, including elephants, and their common ancestor probably dates back to the moment when the African continent split from the other landmasses.

Terrific tunnellers

From grassy plains to woodland scrub, aardvarks enjoy a variety of habitats, but you're unlikely ever to see one 'in the flesh'. That's because they spend much of the day

Comparisons

With their thickset bodies, stocky limbs and long snout, the giant pangolin *(Manis gigantea)* of west Africa resembles an heavily armoured aardvark. Although the two mammals are not related, they have similar body shapes, due to similar lifestyles – both eat termites. Despite their name, giant pangolins are actually smaller than aardvarks. The largest males grow up to 1.4m (4.6ft), although their overlapping scales make them look bulkier.

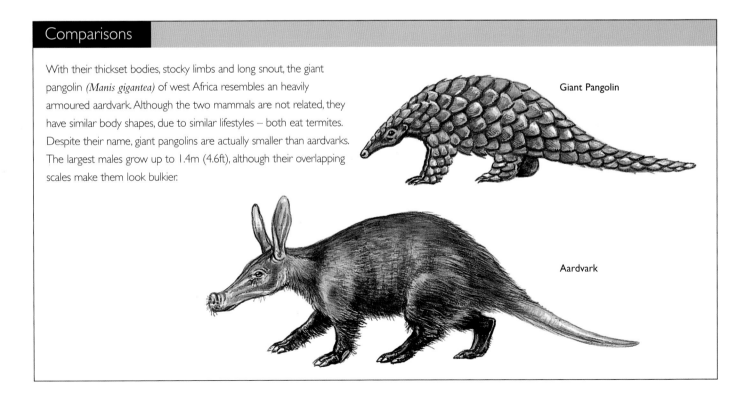

Giant Pangolin

Aardvark

in their burrows, emerging only late in the afternoon or even after sunset. Then they may range up to 30km (18.6 miles) in the search for food – ants, termites and the aardvark cucumber, the only fruit they will eat.

Above ground, aardvarks appear slow and clumsy, but when danger threatens, these cautious creatures can move with surprising speed – bolting for the safety of the nearest subterranean sanctuary. Most aardvarks have several burrows in their territory. Some are just temporary refuges, comprised of a short passageway. Others are extensive tunnel systems connecting several entrances, with a spacious sleeping chamber at one end. Even if an animal is caught away from its burrow, this presents few problems.

Aardvarks are terrific tunnellers and, if trouble strikes, they can dig themselves to safety in a matter of minutes.

When digging, the aardvark rests on its hind legs and tail, pushing the soil under its body with its fore feet and dispersing it with its hind feet. This is such an efficient technique that there are records of one aardvark digging faster than a team of men with shovels! Such a powerful set of claws and paws also make superb defensive weapons. When cornered, these stocky animals can give as good as they get. Tail and claws combined are usually enough to deter all but the hungriest predator. If that doesn't do the trick, the aardvark will often roll onto its back so that it can strike out with all four feet – a killer combination.

Aardvarks are 'nocturnal' and are most active at night. On warm evenings, they emerge from their burrows just after dusk.

Keeping his sensitive nose to the ground, this hungry aardvark patrols the area with a zigzagging motion, until he sniffs out a termite mound.

Powerful claws create a hole in the side of the mound, through which the insects swarm to attack the unwelcome invader.

Up to 45.7cm (18in) long, the aardvark's sticky tongue is its secret weapon – perfect for lapping up termites or ants! The aardvark's thick skin protects it from the insects' stings.

Namib Web-footed Gecko

Despite the extreme heat of Africa's Namib Desert, there's one little lizard that thrives in these energy-draining conditions. But they're not like any lizard you've ever seen. In fact, the translucent skin of these odd geckos make them very difficult to spot at all!

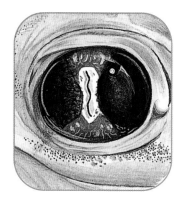

Eyes

Big eyes are designed to gather as much light as possible – invaluable for a species that hunts in the dark.

Mouth

Geckos have no need for large, tearing teeth. Instead, they make do with small, compact teeth to crush insects.

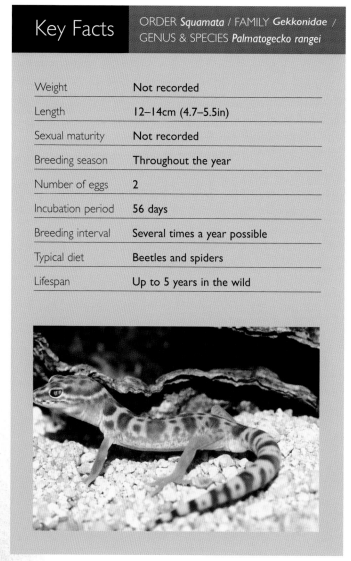

Key Facts

ORDER *Squamata* / FAMILY *Gekkonidae* / GENUS & SPECIES *Palmatogecko rangei*

Weight	Not recorded
Length	12–14cm (4.7–5.5in)
Sexual maturity	Not recorded
Breeding season	Throughout the year
Number of eggs	2
Incubation period	56 days
Breeding interval	Several times a year possible
Typical diet	Beetles and spiders
Lifespan	Up to 5 years in the wild

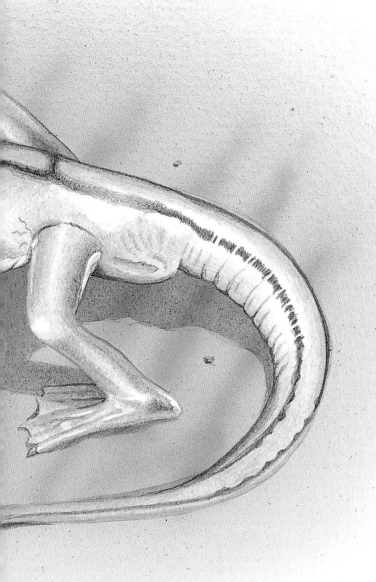

Feet

Fleshy webs act like 'snow shoes', enabling geckos to walk on the surface of the sand without sinking.

We are all shaped by our environment. However, in the sand dunes of south-west Africa there is a species of gecko that has evolved some very unusual characteristics to cope with desert living.

Geckos are found in warm, tropical regions. In Africa alone, there are approximately 41 species. Around eight are found in the area of the Namib–Naukluft National Park, part of the Namib Desert, which is thought to be the world's oldest desert. Many of these are arboreal species and have famously bristly feet, which enable them to 'stick' to almost any surface. As their name suggests, though, Namib web-footed geckos have their own special adaptation to survive in the desert sands.

Unlike their tree-dwelling cousins, web-footed geckos don't need to be able to cling to vertical surfaces (although

they are still good climbers). Instead, their feet are designed to spread their weight so that they don't sink into the sand. Their webbed feet also have an handy, extra 'feature'. They contain small cartilages – stiff connecting tissues – that support a complex system of muscles. These allow the geckos' feet to make highly coordinated movements. So, to escape the baking heat of the midday sun, they simply chill out in burrows that they've specially dug for the purpose. Their foot design makes them superb tunnellers, and these burrows can be up to 50cm (19.7in) long.

Our web-footed friends also have several other physical adaptations that make them real desert specialists. Most geckos, especially the stunningly vibrant day geckos *(genus Phelsuma),* are extremely colourful and, ironically, this helps them to blend in with the rich colours of the rainforest. In

Caught in the open, this web-footed gecko adopts a defensive posture, emitting loud clicks and croaks to intimidate the approaching predator.

Undeterred, the hungry hyena makes a grab for the little lizard, only to be left with a tail-end titbit: the gecko has dropped its tail in self-defence.

All geckos have the capacity to detach their tails and, for this gecko, it turns out to be a life-saving ability.

While the hyena munches down the detached tail, the gecko survives to live another day – and grow another tail!

Comparisons

Apart from skinks *(family Scincidae)*, geckos are one of the most diverse groups in the reptile kingdom. There may be as many as 900 separate species and they come in all sizes. The two smallest are dwarf geckos – *Sphaerodactylus ariasae* and *Sphaerodactylus parthenopion* – which are both less than 1cm (0.4in) long. That's 14 times smaller than the biggest web-footed gecko!

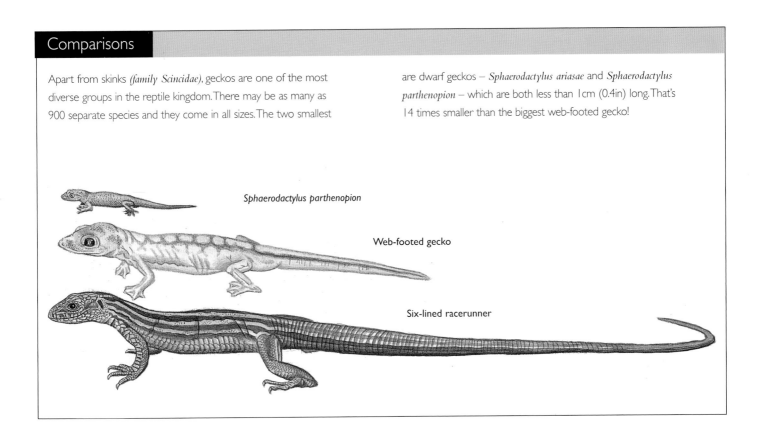

Sphaerodactylus parthenopion

Web-footed gecko

Six-lined racerunner

contrast, web-footed geckos have thin, almost translucent, pink skin, which makes them virtually invisible when viewed against the dusky desert sands.

Strange sights

According to John Heywood's book of proverbs (1546) 'All cats are grey in the dark.' It's a saying that holds true for humans. We see poorly in the dark – generally just fuzzy tones of black and white. So it's easy to imagine that geckos would have a hard time finding their way around at night. Not so. New research has revealed that they may see better in the dark than we do.

All geckos have extremely large eyes to gather as much light as possible. Those species that are active during the day tend to have rounded pupils, but nocturnal reptiles, like the web-footed gecko, have vertical pupils. By day, these pupils narrow to tiny slits to protect the sensitive retina at the back of the eye from damage. According to researchers from Lund University, Sweden, this 'design' has other advantages too. It seems that slit pupils allow those animals with colour vision to see sharply focused images at night – something that no human can do.

Light travels at different wave lengths depending on its colour. Human eyes have single-focus lenses, which means that not every colour is in focus when it hits the lens. Many animals solve this problem with multi-focus lenses, where different parts of the lens are 'tuned in' to different

Namib web-footed gecko habitats

wave lengths. With round pupils, parts of the lens is covered every time the pupil expands or contracts. With a slit pupil, the whole diameter of the lens remains uncovered, allowing every colour to stay in focus. What's more, according to specialist work on nocturnal vision, colour vision is much more common in the animal kingdom than was once assumed, and geckos probably have excellent colour, as well as night, vision.

Giraffe

Standing tall amongst the grasses of Africa's great, sun-parched savannahs, giraffes are an impressive, and extraordinary, sight. With their bold, leopard-print coats, camel-like head, horns, stubby tail, long legs and phenomenal necks, these astounding animals really do have to be seen to be believed.

Tongue and Lips
A blue tongue, which is 53cm (20.8in) long, and flexible lips, are used to pluck leaves off the thorn trees.

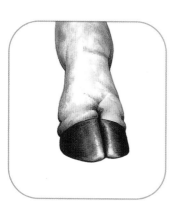

Legs and Hooves
Long, powerful legs are used to lash out at predators. Hooves are cloven (split) and leave a distinctive square-toed print.

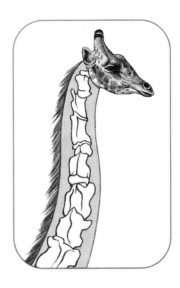

Neck

Most mammals have seven cervical vertebrae (neck bones), regardless of their size. Those in the giraffes' neck are extremely large.

Key Facts	ORDER *Artiodactyla* / FAMILY *Giraffidae* / GENUS & SPECIES *Giraffa camelopardalis*
Weight	Males: 800–1930kg (1763.8–4254.9lb) Females: 550–1180kg (1212.5–2601.4lb)
Length	Males: Up to 5.5m (18ft) Females: up to 4.5m (14.8ft)
Sexual maturity	4–5 years
Breeding season	All year
Number of young	1; occasionally twins
Gestation period	15 months
Breeding interval	Females become receptive every 2 weeks
Typical diet	Leaves and buds
Lifespan	Up to 25 years in the wild; 28 in captivity

Take one look at a giraffe, and it's easy to see why the Romans named them 'camel leopards'. Their heads and long legs do have a camel-like shape, while their spotted coat is reminiscent of that worn by the leopard *(Panthera pardus)*. However, Arab peoples had an even more appropriate name – *ziraafa,* meaning 'assemblage of animals', which is exactly what they look like! The short, brush-ended tail, for instance, could well belong to a warthog *(Phacochoerus africanus).* The long tongue seems to be more appropriate for a reptile, like a chameleon, than a mammal. Indeed, it's so long that they use their tongues to wipe off any bugs that land on their face. Add to this mix a set of cloven hooves (like pigs), a pair of stubby horns and that enormously long neck, and these animals really

For a giraffe, being born can be a traumatic experience. Babies emerge head first and fall to earth with a thud!

As the birth sac breaks open, the young giraffe tumbles, head-first, up to 2m (6.6ft) to the ground!

Undaunted, the newborn looks around, while his mother gets busy cleaning him up with her long, mobile tongue.

Despite his dramatic entrance into the world, he is quickly on his feet and ready to take his first shaky steps.

do look like they are made from bits and pieces taken from other beasts.

Such an eclectic mix of body parts has, however, made the giraffe one of the African savannah's great success stories. A long neck means that they can feed on foliage not accessible to other animals. Their prehensile (gripping) tongue and mobile lips enable them to pull hard to reach buds and leaves into the mouth with ease. Their coat provides them with superb cryptic camouflage, so they can blend in with the dry grasses of the African plains. Their hooves are powerful enough to crush the skull of a lion or break its spine, although giraffes are rarely bothered by predators. Instead, their long legs simply carry them out of trouble at speeds of up to 56km/h (35mph).

Their closest relatives – the okapi *(Okapia johnstoni)* – are equally odd. Their front half resembles a short, brown giraffe. The back looks like a zebra!

Tall tales

Thanks to their long legs and elongated necks, giraffes are the world's tallest mammals. The tallest-ever giraffe measured in at 6m (19.7ft), but an average is between 4.4m and 5.4m (14.8-18ft). Almost half of this is made up of the animal's extraordinary neck, which can be up 2.4m (8ft) in length and weigh up to 272kg (599.6lb). Legs account for another 2m (6.6ft) of this record-breaking bulk; the front legs are slightly longer than the hind legs.

What is so remarkable about these great beasts is that these enormous necks contain only seven vertebrae. That's the same as in humans. Of course, each vertebrae can measure up to 25.4cm (10in) long! Even more incredible is that each vertebrae is bound together with ball-and-socket joints. In humans, such joints link our arms to our shoulders. These giants make giraffes' necks not just long but very flexible.

The reason for the development of such an extraordinary physique has been the subject of much scientific debate. Some argue that it's an adaptation for feeding on the tall arcacia trees that form such an important part of the giraffes' diet. Others believe that long necks form part of the giraffes' sexual display, because males use them like clubs in the mating season to slug it out with rivals. Whatever the reason, in each case, giraffes with the longest necks would have more food and more mates and so be more likely to survive to produce long-necked offspring.

However, long necks haven't been all good news for the giraffe. They need a massive heart and a highly specialized cardiovascular system just to pump blood from their body up to their head!

Giraffe habitats

Comparisons

No one knows for sure how many subspecies of giraffe there are, but each animal has its own, distinct markings, like fingerprints. Reticulated giraffes *(Giraffa camelopardalis reticulata)* have large, polygonal liver-coloured spots, defined by bright, white lines. Rothschild's giraffes *(Giraffa camelopardalis rothschildi)* tend to have deep brown blotches or rectangular spots. And Maasai giraffes *(Giraffa camelopardalis tippelskirchi)* have jagged-edged spots of chocolate-brown on a cream-yellow background.

Maasai giraffe

Hoopoe

With their dramatic head crest and striking plumage, it's no wonder that hoopoes have inspired so many myths and legends. Yet these beautiful birds have one unenviable and strange claim to fame. While other birds preen and clean, hoopoes revel in muck and mess!

Crest
The hoopoes' dramatic crest is flat at rest, but it can be raised when the bird is alarmed or excited.

Feet
Hoopoes have anisodactyl feet, with three toes facing forwards and one facing backwards. This is common for perching birds.

Juvenile
Young hoopoes take some time to develop the characteristic elongated, curved bill, long tail and impressive crest worn by adults.

Key Facts

	ORDER *Coraciiformes* / FAMILY *Upupidae* / GENUS & SPECIES *Upupa epops*
Weight	46–89g (1.6–3.1oz)
Length	25–29cm (9.8–11.4in)
Wingspan	44–48cm (17.3–18.9 in)
Sexual maturity	Few months after fledging
Breeding season	April–Sept, but varies across range
Number of eggs	7–8 eggs; up to 12 in warmer regions
Incubation period	15–16 days
Breeding interval	Yearly
Typical diet	Large insects and small reptiles
Lifespan	Up to 10 years in the wild

Comparisons

Worldwide, there are approximately nine subspecies of hoopoe. These beautiful birds can be found from northern Europe to east Asia, but it's in Africa that they're most at home. Hoopoes are happiest with bare earth beneath their feet and cavities to nest in, which allows them to enjoy a wide range of habitats. Their cousins, the wood-hoopoes, are much choosier, preferring open woodland and savannah.

Wood-hoopoe

Hoopoe

Hoopoe habitats

Dirt brings disease, which is why no sensible bird would ever foul its own nest, but hoopoes seem to positively adore dung!

These odd birds build their nests in cavities, usually in trees or rock faces, although any suitably sized hole will do. Hoopoes have even been found nesting in pipes, discarded burrows and termite mounds. Yet, despite their elegant and refined appearance, they are terrible house-keepers. In fact, it's easy to hunt out a hoopoe nest because they smell so bad!

Breeding females and their chicks produce a foul liquid from their preen gland, which is said to smell like rotting flesh. Added to that, the birds excrete waste directly into the nest, and the blue eggs are very dirty by the time the chicks hatch. The chicks also foul the nest, so by the time they are ready to fly, their homes, and often the birds themselves, are alive with ticks, flies and maggots. No wonder that some people call these birds hoop-poos!

However, this strangely slovenly behaviour may have a serious purpose. Animals live in a rich, sensory world where smells are commonly used to communicate, to mark territory or find a mate. Many animals also use strong smells to deter predators. Skunks, Tasmanian devils, wolverines and stink badgers are some of the most famous mammalian 'stinkers', but a number of birds follow the hoopoes' example. Fulmars *(Fulmarus glacialis)*, for instance, famously projectile vomit a foul-smelling, fishy oil over intruders! But surely hoopoes are only inviting disease by failing to clean away their own excrement? No one knows for sure, but it's been suggested that there's method to their apparent madness. By attracting insects, they ensure that their young have a ready supply of food, exactly where they need it most – in the nest.

Myths and magic

Despite their unsavoury habits, hoopoes have inspired story-tellers and myth makers for thousands of years.

In Ancient Egypt these unmistakable birds were reputedly kept as pets, and they crop up with charming regularly in tomb paintings. On the walls of the flat-topped mastaba of Mereruka at Saqqara, for instance, a hoopoe's nest is shown balanced on a papyrus petal. In the fantastic garden scene, painted on the tomb of Khnumhotep III at Beni Hasan, there's an even lovelier image of a hoopoe, shown in vivid, living colours perched on an acacia tree.

In Greek myth, the hoopoe features in many stories, including the tragic tale of Tereus, Procne and Philomele. In this grim legend, Tereus rapes his wife's sister, Philomele, and then cuts out her tongue to ensure her silence. Philomele manages to smuggle a message to her sister, and together the women plot a hideous revenge. Killing Tereus' own son, they feed the boy's flesh to him during a night of drunken revelry. Enraged, Tereus attacks the women, but the gods intervene, changing all three into birds. Procne becomes a nightingale, forever singing a song of mourning for her dead son. Philomele becomes a swallow. And Tereus spends eternity being mocked as the showy but slightly comical hoopoe, the bird's crest reminding all who see it of his royal status.

In contrast, Farid ud-Din (1146-1221) immortalized the hoopoe as the wisest of all birds in his classic sequence of Iranian poems, *The Conference of the Birds.* Perhaps the most telling reference to this stinky creature, though, comes from the Old Testament. Leviticus 11.13-19 and Deuteronomy 14:11 list all the animals that are considered unclean to eat, including the hoopoe. Which, when you consider its dirty habits, makes very good sense indeed!

These colourful birds often stun their prey by beating it against the ground or a favourite stone. Occasionally, larger animals are subdued by repeated pecking.

Hoopoes prefer to hunt on the ground, where food is more plentiful. Insect larvae are their main prey, but even lizards are easily dealt with.

The hoopoe's downwards-curved bill is an especially useful 'tool'. It can grow up to 5cm (2in) long – ideal for probing the earth for food.

Jackson's Chameleon

Chameleons have earned their place in the annals of the strange thanks to their well-known ability to change their colour to suit their mood. However, Jackson's chameleons have other abilities that are equally strange, which could well qualify these striking reptiles as kings of the bizarre.

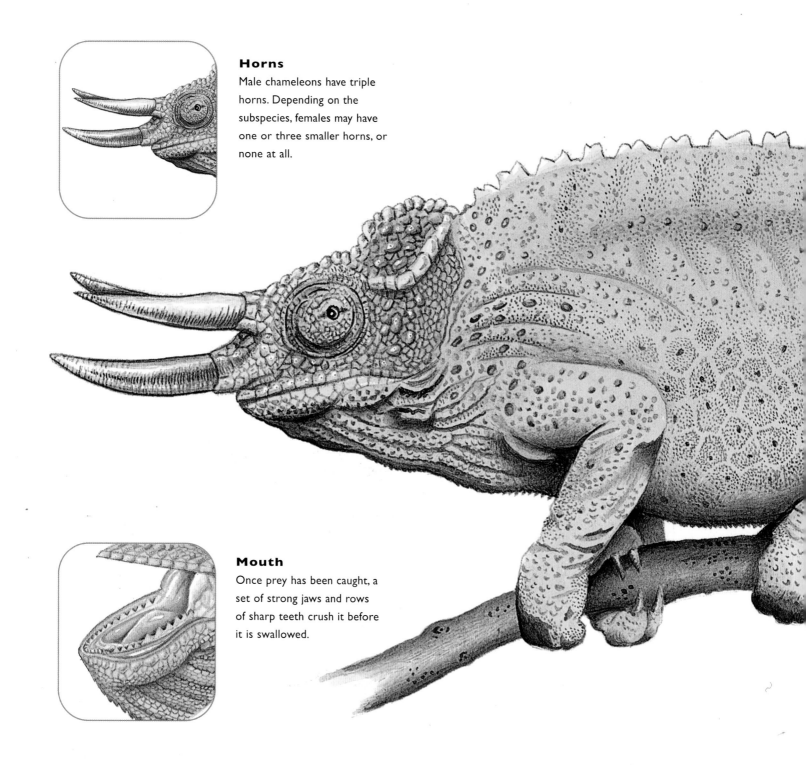

Horns
Male chameleons have triple horns. Depending on the subspecies, females may have one or three smaller horns, or none at all.

Mouth
Once prey has been caught, a set of strong jaws and rows of sharp teeth crush it before it is swallowed.

Tail

A prehensile, gripping tail acts just like a spare pair of hands, helping the chameleon to grip tightly on to branches.

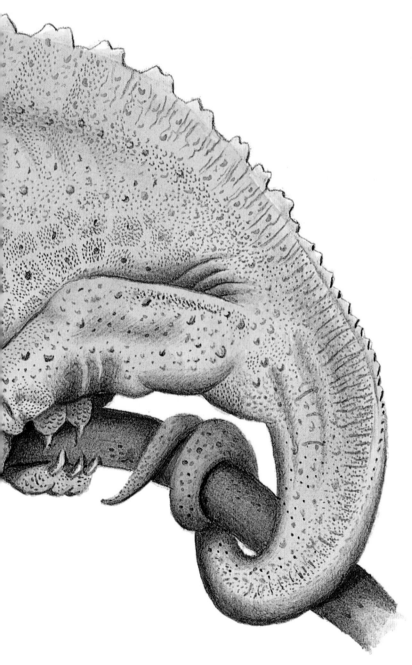

Key Facts

ORDER *Squamata* / FAMILY *Chamaeleontidae* / GENUS & SPECIES *Chamaelo jacksonii*

Weight	Not recorded
Length	20–32cm (7.9–12.6in) including tail
Sexual maturity	5 months
Breeding season	Possibly all year
Number of young	8–30
Gestation period	5–6 months
Breeding interval	Possibly yearly
Typical diet	Small insects
Lifespan	Up to 6 years in the wild; 10 in captivity

Chameleons are perhaps the most well-known of all lizards, although much of their fame is based on a misconception. Their celebrated ability to alter their skin colour happens only in response to variations in the environment or changes in the reptiles' mood, not as a direct attempt to blend in with their surroundings. Nevertheless, how chameleons change their colour is a fascinating process and it all starts, sensibly enough, in the skin.

Chameleons have four layers of skin. First comes the nether layer, which can reflect the colour white. On top of that is the melanophore layer, which contains the dark pigment melanin, meaning that brown and black can be produced. This layer also reflects blue. Next comes the chromatophore layer, which contains yellow and red pigments. Finally there's the outer, protective layer of the skin, called the epidermis.

When chameleons become warm or cold, or feel scared or excited, chemical changes in their body cause the colour-carrying cells in these layers of skin to expand or shrink. This creates a blend of colours as each layer produces its own distinct patterns and shades. Often these colour changes are used purely for display, to help the males attract a mate. At other times, such changes are used as defensive camouflage. However, contrary to popular belief, chameleons can't choose what colour they want to be. Nor do they have a limitless palette to select from. So, if we were to place one of these strange lizards on a striped scarf, it wouldn't automatically blend in with its

Jackson's chameleon habitats

new habitat. It might change colour because it felt threatened or because the scarf was hot or wet, but the colours it could produce would be limited – and not especially stripy!

Seriously strange

Many of us know that chameleons can change colour, but these striking-looking reptiles have other, equally strange characteristics that make them unique.

Comparisons

Chameleons come in all sizes, from the 3.3cm (1.3in) dwarf *Brookesia minima* to the 68.5cm (27in) Malagasy giant *(Furcifer oustaleti)*. Despite this, their bodies are similar, although many species sport striking head decorations. Some, like Jackson's

chameleon have dramatic horns. The crested chameleon *(Chamaeleo cristatus)* has rows of bumps. And the veiled chameleon *(Chamaeleo calyptratus)* is the most showy of all, thanks to its helmet-like casque.

Jackson's Chameleon

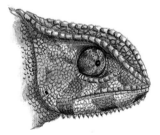

Crested Chameleon

Veiled Chameleon

A chameleon's ability to change colour is its first line of defence, although the colours it can use are limited.

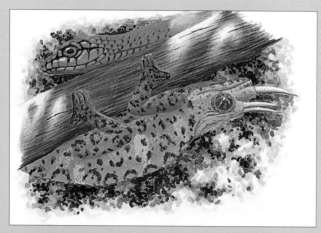

Chameleons can't exactly match their surroundings but, in the jungle, bold patterns and shades still make a good disguise!

As the snake presses its attack, our chameleon resorts to intimidation – hissing and posturing aggressively, with its mouth wide open.

The snake is still unimpressed, so our chameleon makes a speedy exit, releasing his grip and dropping onto a branch below.

Chameleons can be found throughout Africa's humid, forest regions and so, not surprisingly, their bodies have adapted to a life spent amongst the tree tops. They have a gripping (prehensile) tail, which acts a little like a fifth arm to help steady them as they creep through the forest. Their bulging eyes can rotate to give them a full 360° view of the environment. Each eye is also able to focus separately. That means that they can look at two different objects at the same time – a very useful skill when navigating through the gloomy forest canopy!

Look at the chameleons' feet, and you'll notice something even odder – they're zygodactyl. Birds like parrots have zygodactyl feet, where two of their toes point backwards, and two forwards. This is an evolutionary adaptation that enables them to hold onto

branches. Although chameleons have five toes, not four, their feet work in the same way as a parrots, enabling them to hold onto foliage with a vicelike grip.

Then there's the chameleon's tongue. Many reptiles have long, thin or forked tongues. In contrast, chameleon tongues are big and fleshy. Their bodies may be slow, but these powerful, elongated tongues shoot out of the chameleon's mouth at incredible speeds, catching prey on the sticky tip and pulling them into the mouth, enveloped in a ball of muscle.

Finally, these beautiful lizards have one more surprise to reveal. Most reptiles lay eggs, but the Jackson's chameleon are viviparous and give birth to live young – making them a true oddity in a world of oddities.

Naked Mole Rat

There's more to the naked mole rat than meets the eye. Their hairless bodies make them look extremely odd, but it's only once you get to know the habits of these rodents of east African that you realize just how curious these creatures really are.

Key Facts	ORDER *Rodentia* / FAMILY *Bathyergidae* / GENUS & SPECIES *Heterocephalus glaber*	
Weight	30–35g (1–1.2oz) Queens: up to 80g (2.8oz)	
Length	10–13cm (3.9–5.1in) including tail	
Sexual maturity	Only dominant female breeds	
Breeding season	All year	
Number of young	12–24	
Gestation period	66–74 days	
Breeding interval	Up to 4 litters a year	
Typical diet	Roots and vegetation	
Lifespan	Up to 30 years in the wild	

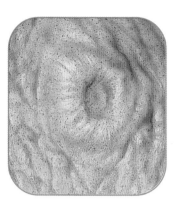

Ears

Although they appear to have no ears, mole rats have good hearing. The fleshy, external part of the ear is missing, probably to avoid damage when the rats are tunnelling.

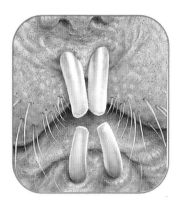

Teeth

Mole rats use these over-sized incisors to dig, so they have to be strong and well rooted. The lips are sealed just behind the teeth to stop soil entering their mouths.

Many burrowing animals live in large family groups, but naked mole rats have a system that makes them almost unique in the mammal world. Their large, underground 'nests' contain up to 300 individuals, but only one female produces young. This is called eusociality.

Just like in a bee hive, this 'queen' dominates and controls the entire group. However, the queen bee is the only fertile female in a hive. Mole rat communities contain fertile members of both sexes. The queen mole rat maintains her supremacy, and stops other females from breeding, using chemical warfare! Her urine contains pheromones that surpress the urge to breed. She's also a merciless bully, and a combination of stress and intimidation play a part in keeping other females in line.

The queen may have up to three mates and produces as many as four litters a year. As soon as her pups are grown, they join her army of workers — and it seems that every new worker has a specific job to do. Some are tunnellers, responsible for maintaining and adding to the burrow's passageways, nest chambers, food stores, defecation sites and bolt holes. Some are soldiers, who protect the group from predators. Some are even 'farmers', who create and maintain the nests' self-renewing food stores. They do this by removing just part of a root or tuber, then sealing them up in a special chamber until they've regrown.

Although ant, termite and some bee communities all form eusocial societies, it's unusual to find mammals living in such structured and hierarchical groups. The only

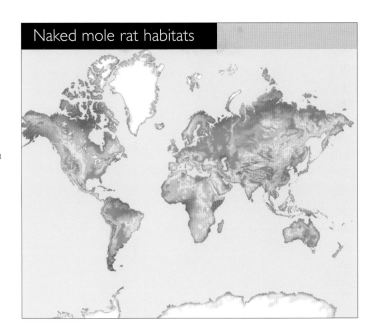

Naked mole rat habitats

other mammals to do so are the Damaraland mole rats *(Cryptomys damarensis)*, which live in sub-Saharan Africa.

Subterranean specialists

All successful animals adapt to make the most of their environment — and the naked mole rat is a true subterranean specialist. Just one look at these weird and wonderful creatures tells us that they're built for tunnelling. Their low-set, streamlined bodies, small eyes

Comparisons

The Cape dune mole rat, native to the dunes and plains of South Africa, is the largest member of the mole rat family, weighing 16 times more than the naked mole rat, with a body length of more than 30cm

(12in). Despite the difference in size and coat, these two mole rat species have a remarkably similar body shape — a reflection of their similar burrowing lifestyles.

Cape dune mole rat

Naked mole rat

and almost invisible, 'sealed' ears aren't unique. Similar adaptations can be found in almost any burrowing mammal. But, when it comes to surviving beneath the thorn tree savannah of east Africa, naked mole rats have some extra tricks up their sleeves.

These amazing rodents live in narrow tunnels, up to 1.8m (6ft) below the ground. In such stuffy and poorly ventilated conditions, there is little oxygen available and the air the mole rats breathe is so often so toxic that it would kill other mammals. Mole rats are able to survive and thrive thanks to thousands of years of evolution. During this time, their lungs have shrunk and their blood has become especially good at binding oxygen, allowing them to breathe much more efficiently. A study at the University of Illinois, Chicago, USA, found that, without oxygen, mouse brains could 'survive' for about 3 minutes only, while the mole rat brain could function for up to 30 minutes!

Living in such toxic surroundings has had other, interesting, side effects too. Naked mole rats have an amazingly slow metabolic rate and use very little energy to stay alive. Most strange of all, though, is that these wrinkly rodents don't feel chemically induced pain. Acid could be split on their skin and they wouldn't notice! Researchers have discovered that they lack a common neuro-transmitter called Substance P. Surprisingly, this brings an advantage: high levels of carbon dioxide build up within their burrows, and this is a gas that is acidic. So, because they lack Substance P, mole rats are easily able to endure the toxic, acidic air of their burrows without discomfort.

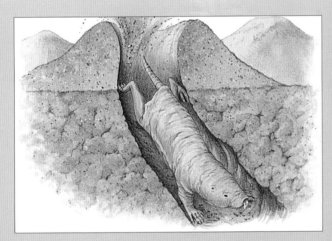

An amazing 25 per cent of the mole rat's musculature is in their jaws, allowing them to cut through compacted earth with ease.

Some of the most elaborate tunnel systems measure more than 3km (1.9 miles) long, meaning that mole rats must work together.

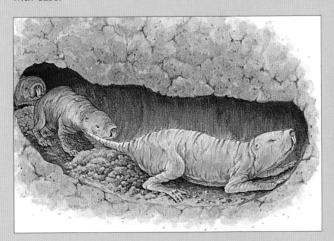

While one tunneller slices away the earth, others help to remove the loose soil, which would otherwise block the passageway.

Digging a tunnel may be easy, but navigating through narrow passageways can be a tricky process, especially if someone else wants to get past!

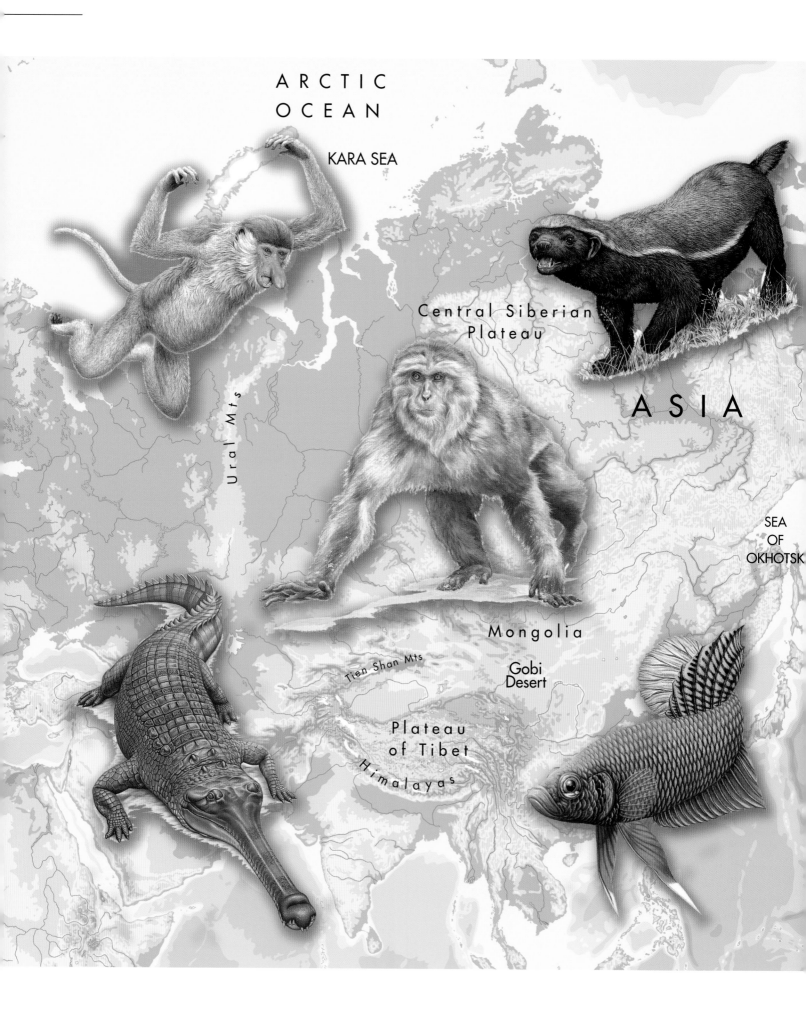

ARCTIC
OCEAN

KARA SEA

Central Siberian
Plateau

ASIA

Ural Mts

SEA
OF
OKHOTSK

Mongolia

Tien Shan Mts

Gobi
Desert

Plateau
of Tibet

Himalayas

Asia

Across the vast continent of Asia can be found the world's highest mountains and, in their shadow, one of its largest deserts. To the south-east lie some of the world's largest and most populated islands.

~

Unlike the other continents, Asia has no obvious border to mark its boundaries. In fact, Europe is no longer considered a separate continent from Asia. The region we call Asia is a spectacular, sprawling landmass, and it is perhaps no surprise that sixty per cent of the world's population – around four billion people – make their home here.

This is the world's largest continent. And it is truly amazing. Look east and there, sandwiched between China and Siberia, we see the vast Gobi Desert: a parched rain shadow desert created by the Himalayan mountains, which stop moisture reaching this weather-wizened land. Glance west and we find the highest region in the world, known as 'High Asia' or 'the roof of the world' – a place of gigantic peaks and deep valleys where Afghanistan, Pakistan and China collide. Travel south, and you'll find some of the world's densest rainforests, stretching from Myanmar and the Philippines and across the North China Sea to Indonesia. This is a nation comprised of 17,508 inspirational islands, which play host to more species of animals and plant life than anywhere else in the world, apart from the Amazon rainforest.

It's this geological diversity that makes Asia home to some of the world's rarest, most beautiful and most exciting animals. Pandas, tigers and elephants all find a home here. So too do some of nature's strangest and most surprising species. It's here that you'll come across monkeys that take shelter from the winter cold in hot springs, and fish that can not only survive out of water but are even able to walk across the land.

Gharial

With their thin, elongated snout and delicate, light-weight skull, gharials are one of the most odd-looking members of the crocodilian family. Despite their reputation as man-eaters, though, their strangely shaped snout tells a different tale. These awesome reptiles are piscivores – eating fish, rather than people!

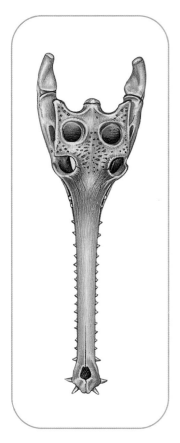

Snout

Male and female gharials are sexually dimorphic and differ in size and appearance. Males can be recognized thanks to a characteristic, bulbous growth on the tip of the snout.

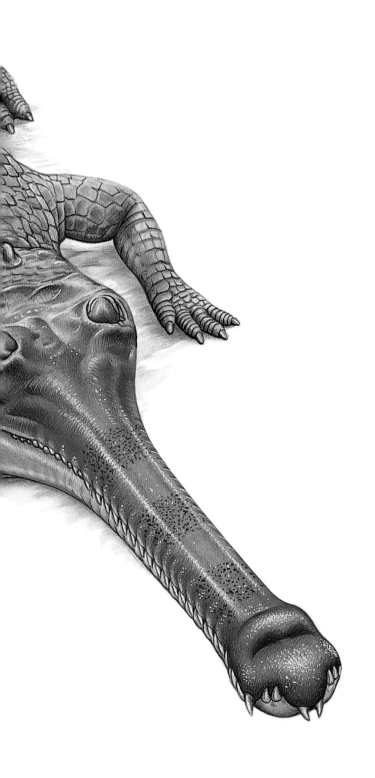

Key Facts

	ORDER *Crocodylia* / FAMILY *Gavialidae* / GENUS & SPECIES *Gavialis gangeticus*
Weight	Average: 977kg (2153.9lb)
Length	Average: 3.6–4.5m (11.8–15.8ft)
Sexual maturity	10 years
Breeding season	November–January
Number of eggs	30–50
Incubation period	83–94 days
Breeding interval	Yearly
Typical diet	Young eat insects; adults eat fish
Lifespan	40–60 years in the wild

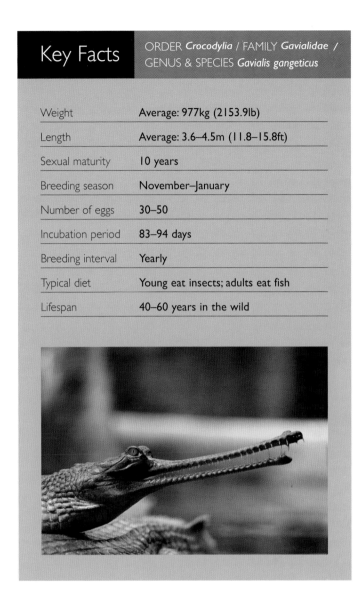

Feet

These distinctive reptiles propel themselves through water using their webbed feet and long hind legs. Their long, flattened tail helps them to steer and adds stability.

More people in Africa are killed by hippopotami than by crocodiles, but these incredible creatures still generate fear and awe wherever they're encountered. And rightly so. Crocodiles may rarely attack people, but these mighty, muscled meat-eaters are one of nature's most perfectly adapted hunters.

Perhaps the biggest and most notorious member of this reptile family are Nile crocodiles *(Crocodylus niloticus)*. These powerful animals are the largest crocodilians in Africa and the third largest, worldwide, after the saltwater crocodile *(Crocodylus porosus)* and the gharial. On average, all three species rarely grow beyond 5m (16.4ft) in length. With enough food and time, though, they may top the 6m (19.7ft) mark. And the largest gharial, shot in northern Bihar in 1924, was a staggering 7m (23ft) long, from the tip of his bulbous snout to the tapering end of his armoured tail.

Nile and saltwater crocodiles are quite capable of attacking anything that wanders into their territory – and they often do. But people have little to fear from the gharial. It may be one of the 'big boys', but it is not, in fact, a man-eater. It is simply not equipped for such dirty work.

An adult gharial's preferred food is fish, and its jaws and teeth are perfectly adapted for such a diet. These patient predators spend much of their day in the river, lying low and waiting to grab passing prey with a swift, sideways sweep of the head. Their thin snout gives them

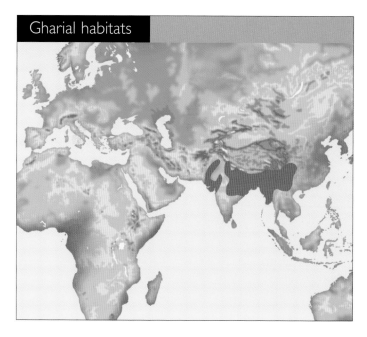

Gharial habitats

added reach and their slender profile reduces water resistance. Any fish caught this way is held fast, impaled by razor-sharp teeth that lock firmly together. Yet, it's not just the gharials' distinctive snout that makes them such perfect piscivores.

Too specialized?

Crocodilians are an ancient and widespread group of reptile. In fact, they have been so successful as a species that they've changed very little since dinosaurs ruled the

Comparisons

Like its Indian cousin, the false gharial *(Tomistoma schlegelii)* makes its living in freshwater rivers. Currently this rare reptile can be found in Sumatra, Malaysia and a few remote river systems on the island of

Borneo. Its slightly broader snout means that it has a much more adventurous diet than the 'true' gharial, and eats large vertebrates such as monkeys and deer as well as fish.

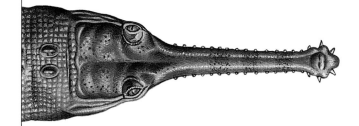

False gharial

Gharial

Clean, fast rivers, with deep pools and sand banks for resting and basking on, are the gharials' favourite hunting grounds.

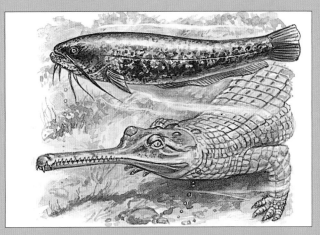

These distinctive-looking crocodiles don't like to hurry. Rather than pursue prey, they prefer to lie in wait for a passing meal.

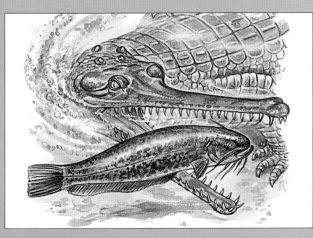

Once this catfish is within easy reach, our cautious crocodile strikes — with open jaws ready to seize the unsuspecting fish.

Its narrow snout is the perfect shape for manipulating slippery fish and, with a few well-judged movements, the catfish is quickly gulped down.

Earth. During this time, their bodies have adapted to suit their habits and habitats. They have a super-efficient four-chambered heart, which enables them to stay submerged for long periods of time. Their throats have a slitlike valve, which closes underwater, so that they can eat without drowning. Their eyes and nostrils are positioned towards the top of their head so that they can see and breathe while the rest of their body lies submerged in the shallows. They also have fantastic eyesight, with vertical pupils that widen in the dark to aid night-time hunting.

However, being a specialist does have its drawbacks. Some crocodilians are equally at home in and out of the water. Nile crocodiles, for instance, are both superb swimmers and alarmingly fast runners. When they need to,

these stocky crocodiles can use their short but strong legs to raise their muscular bodies up off the ground and charge forwards with surprising speed. Gharials, though, are true specialists. Water is their natural element and on land they are so clumsy they can manoeuvre only by dragging their bellies along the ground. Their leg muscles cannot lift their body off the ground. Once they are submerged in fast-flowing waters, though, it's a different story. Their feet possess extensive webbing and their tail is powerful and well developed, with a laterally flattened design that cuts through water with ease. Gharials are so agile in the water that they can even use their bodies to corral fish into the shallows, where they can be more easily snapped up and gulped down.

Japanese Macaque

These beautifully furry 'snow monkeys' display a range of behaviour that is startlingly human, from bathing to baby-sitting, from flavouring their food to snowball fights! In fact, Japanese macaques have become a favourite with researchers thanks to their intelligence and complex social lives.

Teeth

Despite the male's impressive-looking canine teeth, macaques are mainly frugivores (fruit-eaters), although their diet varies through the year.

Hand

Most primates, including humans, have 'opposable thumbs', which are thumbs that can be bent to touch all of the fingers.

Key Facts

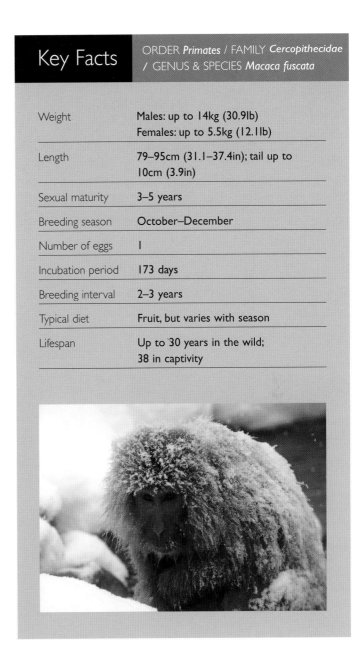

ORDER *Primates* / FAMILY *Cercopithecidae* / GENUS & SPECIES *Macaca fuscata*	
Weight	Males: up to 14kg (30.9lb) Females: up to 5.5kg (12.1lb)
Length	79–95cm (31.1–37.4in); tail up to 10cm (3.9in)
Sexual maturity	3–5 years
Breeding season	October–December
Number of eggs	1
Incubation period	173 days
Breeding interval	2–3 years
Typical diet	Fruit, but varies with season
Lifespan	Up to 30 years in the wild; 38 in captivity

Tail

Japanese macaques live in cold, northerly climates. Their tails are therefore short, which makes them less likely to suffer frostbite.

Many mammals live in highly structured groups, dominated by a single male, who has exclusive breeding rights with the females. He earns these rights by competing with other males, and once he's made it to the top he must spend the rest of his life defending his position from challengers. It's a brutal system and one that macaques have managed to side-step.

These appealing, red-faced monkeys are unusual in that, within their tightly knit troops, males and females have an almost equal relationship. Most troops have a ratio of four females per male, and it's the females who choose when and with whom they want to mate. What's more, macaques seem to enjoy sex for its own sake! Members of the troop mate all year round, not just in the breeding season, and it's not uncommon for a female to have as

many as 10 sexual partners during the year. It's not just their attitude to sex that makes macaque society unusual, either. Both males and females take turns to care for the young and even grandparents will get involved and step in to feed and look after babies who have been abandoned or orphaned.

Despite this, life in a macaque troop isn't always peaceful and co-operative! Just like in the human world, some macaques are more successful than others. The bathing monkeys of Jigokudani (Hell's Valley) Monkey Park have a better quality of life than the macaques who live on the outskirts of the cities, where food is scarce and competition for resources is intense. In these troops, lifespans are shorter, illness is rife and aggression between troop members is more common. Individual monkeys

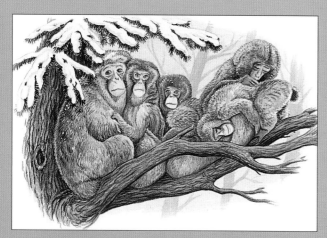

Winters in northern Japan can be bitterly cold. Fortunately, macaques have learnt that hot springs are an ideal way to keep out a chill.

Almost 50 years ago, macaques in Jigokudani (Hell's Valley) were lured by food to the hot, volcanic springs that give the area its name.

The troop quickly leant to appreciate both the free food and the warm waters and have visited the site every day since, returning to the safety of the forests at night.

Despite its remote location, 90,000 human visitors also trek through the woods to catch a glimpse of these famous, water-loving primates.

Comparisons

Rhesus monkeys *(Macaca mulatta)* – also known as Rhesus macaques – are natives of Afghanistan, Bangladesh, Burma, China, northern India, Pakistan and Thailand. Like Japanese macaques, they are Old World monkeys and share many physical characteristics with their cousins. They're a similar size, though less bulky. As their natural habitats are warmer, their fur is shorter and their tails are longer, being less prone to frostbite.

Rhesus monkey

Japanese macaque

even show symptoms of stress similar to those found in their human, city-dwelling counterparts.

Look and learn

It's thanks to macaques that scientists have begun to re-think their ideas about monkey 'societies'. These intelligent primates enjoy an extremely complex social life, and it's one that is constantly changing and evolving. The bathing macaques of Jigokudani are a case in point.

The springs in this region are natural, but it wasn't until 1963 that a young female macaque, named Mukubili, decided to try them out for herself. Although she was initially tempted into the warm waters by some soybeans, thrown in by keepers of the Park, she obviously liked the experience. She came back again and again, and other macaques eventually followed suit. Thanks to this one incident, the lives of every member of the troop have now changed irrevocably. They come down to the springs when a gong rings to tell them that food is available. Although they're still wild animals, they've become so used to the presence of tourists, that they're quite happy to stay and be observed. They've effectively become monkey celebrities!

Similar adaptive behaviour has been recorded by the Japanese Primate Research Institute on the island of Kojima. Again food (this time sweet potatoes) was used to tempt the macaques into the open, where they could be observed. One female, Imo, found that it was easier to get sand off the potatoes by dipping it into river water, rather than brushing it off with her hands. The trick was quickly learnt – and improved upon – by the rest of the troop. Later, some macaques started to dip their potatoes in sea water. They would bite into them, then dip them in the water, then bite them again, presumably because the potatoes tested better that way!

Japanese macaque habitats

Mudskipper

Down on the water's edge, something strange is stirring. Mudskippers are amphibious fish and spend just as much time out of the water as they do in it. At low tide, they even use their fins like feet to propel themselves across the mud flats!

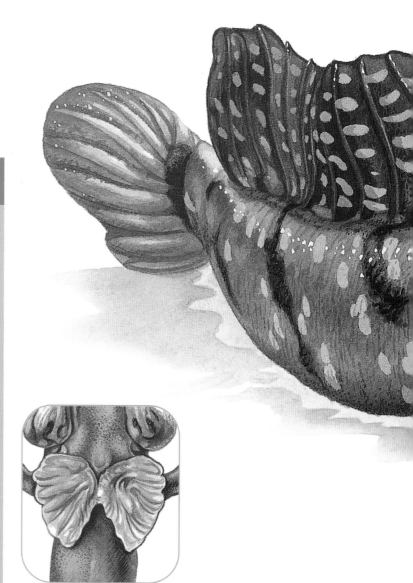

Key Facts	ORDER *Perciformes*/ FAMILY *Gobiidae* / GENUS & SPECIES *Genus periophthalmus*	
Weight	Average: 10g (0.3oz)
Length	Up to 25cm (9.8in), depending on species
Sexual maturity	Average: 2 years
Breeding season	Rainy season
Number of eggs	100–200
Incubation period	14–21 days
Breeding interval	Yearly
Typical diet	Algae or small vertebrates, depending on species
Lifespan	Up to 5 years in the wild

Pelvic fins

These remarkable fish use their fins to 'walk' on land. They can run and jump, and some can even climb using their pelvic fins, which are linked to create a sucker-like appendage.

Eyes

A pair of swivelling eyes are mounted, turret-like, on top of the mudskippers' bulbous head. This enables them to see, above the water even when their bodies are submerged.

Comparisons

All mudskippers can be identified by the size, shape and colour of their fins. The Atlantic mudskipper *(Periophthalmus barbarus)*, for instance, has an elongated dorsal fin, stretching across much of its back. In the gold-spotted mudskipper *(Periophthalmus chrysospilos)*, the dramatic front ray may be twice the height of the fish's body. And the dorsal fin of *Periophthalmus koelreuteri* is curled, making it appear delightfully leaflike.

Atlantic mudskipper   Gold-spotted mudskipper   Periophthalmus koelreuteri

Mudskippers belong to a large, but relatively unstudied group of fish known as gobies. Gobies first appeared on Earth around 30–50 million years ago and, since then, they have become one of the most successful and diverse fish families *(Gobiidae)*. Currently there are thought to be as many as 2000 species, and they can be found all over the world, except in the waters of the Arctic, the Antarctic and the deep oceans. In fact, these strikingly coloured fish prefer life in the shallows. Many make their homes on coral reefs, around sandy shores or on the shallow continental shelves that run along the coasts of Africa, India, south-east Asia and northern Australia.

At some point in the distant past, the ancestors of today's mudskippers moved into even shallower waters, probably to avoid predators as well as to exploit new, untapped food reserves. The descendants of these 'amphibious' fish can now be found on mud flats and in brackish, mangrove swamps, throughout the world's tropical, subtropical and temperate regions. Here, they can often be seen at low tide, skipping and hopping across the water-logged ground. But perhaps the most remarkable thing about these fish is that they don't simply flap around in the shallows like the proverbial fish out of water.

In the water, these bog-eyed beasts swim with side-to-side movements, just like any other gobie, but it's on land that they are at their most astounding. They are incredibly active and agile. They can dig, run, climb,

jump, flip their bodies through the air, and – as their name suggests – they can even skip across land with surprising speed. All this is possible thanks to some very special physical adaptations.

Land lubbers

Any species that moves from water on to land has two major obstacles to overcome: breathing and walking!

Mudskipper habitats

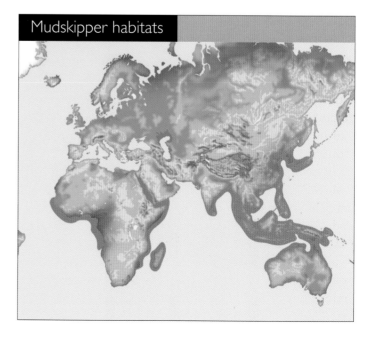

Larger species of mudskippers reproduce on land in purpose-built, funnel-shaped burrows. These need to be deep enough to stay permanently flooded.

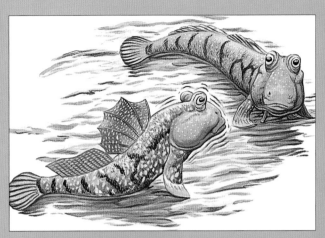

Each male energetically guards his burrow, deterring passing, rival males by bobbing aggressively and flashing his dorsal fins.

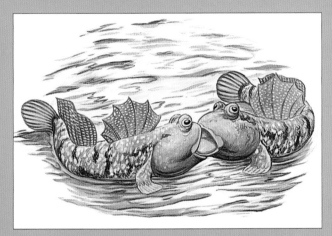

This intruder isn't impressed, so our resident mudskipper tackles the problem head on, locking mouths with the interloper in a trial of strength.

Fortunately, the female is impressed! She follows the victorious male to his burrow, where she lays her eggs in special brooding chambers.

Fish don't breathe water. They need oxygen just like we do, but instead of filtering it out of the air, they use gills to extract it from the water. When fish open and close their mouths, with that slightly comic gulping action, they're actually breathing. They are taking in water and pumping it through their gills, where oxygen and carbon dioxide are exchanged.

Mudskippers have adapted this procedure so that they can continue to extract oxygen from the water while on land. Their enlarged gill chambers can be filled with water and then 'sealed up'. As long as these chambers are refilled regularly, their gills will continue to work extracting oxygen. If they stay wet, they can also absorb oxygen through their skin just like amphibians. By combining both systems, mudskippers can stay on land for up to three days.

Moving about on land with only fins, rather than legs, has necessitated further, subtle adaptations. Many aquatic gobies already have vertical fins, which are fused into a cup shape. These help them to cling onto coral. Some species of mudskippers use the same 'adhesive cups' to climb around on the mud flats in search of food. Others use these unfused fins like hind legs. The mudskippers' secret to success, though, are their enlarged pectoral fins.

Pectoral fins are located on either side of a fishes' body and, in aquatic species, they help to generate 'lift' as the fish swim. Mudskippers use them in conjunction with their strong caudal tail fins, enabling them to walk, quite effectively, with a hopping, jerky gait known as crutching.

Proboscis Monkey

It's hard to ignore such a sizeable snout! A male proboscis monkey's nose can be up to 18cm (7in) long, although such prodigious protuberances are nothing compared to their stomachs! Yet, it's what's going on inside these big bellies that's really strange.

Juveniles

Young proboscis monkeys look little like their parents, with brilliantly blue faces, blackish fur and a relatively normal-sized nose.

Key Facts	ORDER *Primates* / FAMILY *Cercopithecidae* / GENUS & SPECIES *Nasalis larvatus*	
Weight	Males: 20–24kg (44.1–52.9lb) Females: 10–12 kg (22–26.4lb)
Length	Males: 73–76cm (28.7–29.9in). Females: 60–64cm (23.6–25.2in), excluding tail
Sexual maturity	4–5 years
Breeding season	All year
Number of young	1
Gestation period	166–200 days
Breeding interval	All year
Typical diet	Leaves and fruit
Lifespan	Up to 13 years in the wild; 25 in captivity

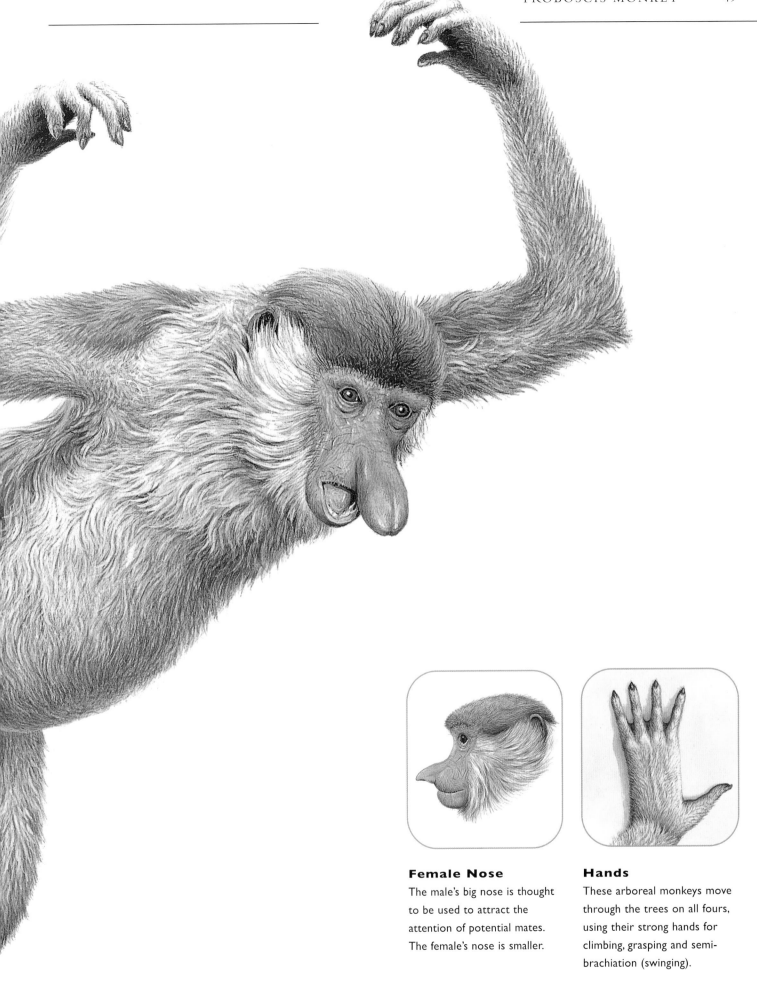

Female Nose

The male's big nose is thought to be used to attract the attention of potential mates. The female's nose is smaller.

Hands

These arboreal monkeys move through the trees on all fours, using their strong hands for climbing, grasping and semi-brachiation (swinging).

Proboscis monkey habitats

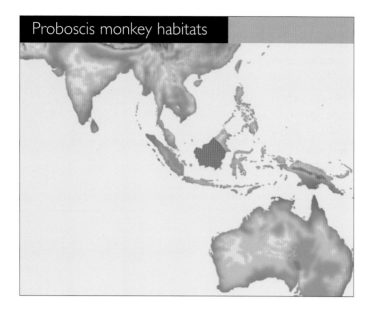

When Dutch settlers arrived in Indonesia in the 1600s, the locals noticed something that made them laugh. Many of the new arrivals had big noses and big bellies, just like the native monkeys. And that is why one of the local nicknames for the proboscis monkey is orang belanda, which means 'Dutchman'!

Undoubtedly the most prominent feature of these reddish-brown primates are their huge, extended noses.

These amazing proboscises can be up to 18cm (7in) long and hang down over the mouth like a deflated balloon. Only the males have such large noses. Females have smaller, more delicate protuberances, although they're still big for primates. However, in the world of the proboscis monkey, size is everything. The bigger the male's nose, the more attractive he appears to the opposite sex.

Water Lovers

Unlike most primates, proboscis monkeys are just as comfortable in the water as in the tree tops – they even have partially webbed feet. These water-lovers therefore make their homes around flooded, lowland swamps where a wide range of food can be found. Such wetlands may provide easy pickings for a hungry herbivore, but they can also be dangerous places to live. When trouble strikes, proboscis monkeys will often drop into the water and swim to safety, but this isn't always a good plan! One of the species' main predators are false gharials *(Tomistoma schlegelii)*, which often take immature monkeys from the water and will even pluck them from low branches. Luckily, that big nose has other uses besides attracting a mate. It works like an echo chamber, enabling males to produce startlingly loud honking sounds to warn off predators. When they're especially agitated, their nose swells with blood, producing louder and deeper calls.

Comparisons

Although they're both Old World primates, proboscis monkeys and golden snub-nosed monkeys *(Rhinopithecus roxellana)* couldn't look more different. The snub-nosed species are slightly smaller with rich, yellow-gold fur and, as their name suggests, small noses. These increasingly rare primates are found in dense forests in the mountains of China. Their big-nosed cousins are also arboreal but prefer wet lowland habitats, swamps and riparian forests close to water.

Snub-nosed monkey

Proboscis monkey

The proboscis monkey's huge nose is so striking that it's easy to overlook their other prominent feature – their big bellies!

These sociable animals live in troops of up to 40, spending much of their time foraging for food and sleeping. A typical day will start with a meal by the water's edge. They'll then move inland to find a cosy spot where they can doze through the warmest part of the day. As the afternoon arrives, the troop will gradually drift back to the riverside where they feed again before night falls.

Proboscis monkeys are mostly folivores and frugivores. They eat leaves and unripe fruit. Seeds, flowers, bark and insects will all be eaten in small amounts as they become available through the year. In total, they enjoy around 90 species of plant, with a 50:50 mix of leaves and fruit.

Due to such a specialized diet, proboscis monkeys and their relatives are known as leaf monkeys. As leaves aren't especially nutritious, members of this group must eat a lot of foliage to stave off hunger. The result is that their stomachs are so large it's impossible to tell if the females are pregnant. In fact, the males look pregnant too! However, within these big bellies something remarkable is going on. To make the most of every mouthful, these stomachs are divided into several compartments, and work in a similar way to the stomachs of ruminants, like cows. In here, bacteria digest cellulose and get rid of the toxins that are contained in many plant foods. (What they can't do, though, is to digest ripe fruit.) This form of digestion is a slow process and the contents of a proboscis monkey's belly can account for up to a quarter of its body weight!

These big-nosed primates make their homes amongst the tree tops of Borneo's lush mangrove forests, steamy swamps and water-logged woodlands.

These distinctive monkeys can move quickly through the trees, but they're just as happy in the water. They are good swimmers, often swimming between islands.

When wading through shallows, they adopt an upright stance, with females carrying babies on their hips to keep them safe.

But even deep waters are no problem for these peculiar primates, especially if a tasty treat lies on the other bank.

Ratel

These cuddly critters may look cute, but they hold a surprising record. According to the 2003 edition of *The Guinness Book of Records,* these boldly patterned beasts are 'the most fearless animals in the world'. They've even had an armoured personnel carrier named after them!

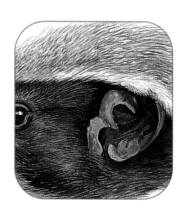

Ears

A pair of handy ear flaps can be closed up when ratels are digging or during raids on bee hives, when tender parts of the animals' body are likely to get stung!

Key Facts	ORDER *Carnivora* / FAMILY *Mustelidae* / GENUS & SPECIES *Mellivora capensis*
Weight	Males: up to 14kg (30.9lb) Females: up to 10 kg (22 lb)
Length	60–102cm (23.6–40.1in) Tail: 16–30cm (6.3–11.8in)
Sexual maturity	Not recorded
Breeding season	8 months
Number of young	1–2
Gestation period	50–70 days
Breeding interval	Twice a year
Typical diet	Large invertebrates, small reptiles, mammals and honey
Lifespan	Up to 9 years in wild; 28 in captivity

Fore feet

The ratels' powerful fore feet come equipped with a set of long, curved claws. These serve as useful digging tools but also make formidable weapons, for both attack or defence.

It may be no bigger than a dog but, according to the record books, the ratel is officially 'the most fearless animal in the world'. According to urban myths, ratels aren't simply efficient hunters but are also man-killers, with a reputation for hamstringing and castrating their victims! Such tales are so widely believed that, in 2007, rumours of British troops releasing 'man-eating badgers' into Basra City, Iraq spread panic amongst the population. It wasn't true – native ratels were simply being driven towards the city because the marsh lands to the north were flooding. Yet, subsequent stories of 'badgers as swift as deer' attacking housewives did little to lessen the reputation of this much maligned mammal.

In truth, there's no concrete evidence that ratels are man-killers, and many of the tales told about these nocturnal wanderers are undoubtedly exaggerations. Nevertheless, they are remarkably tenacious creatures. When threatened, they put up a formidable defence, rushing towards their enemy with a loud, rattling roar. If caught, they can wriggle within their own skin, to bite back – in fact, they have been known to kill the animals that have attacked them, including lions and bears. As hunters, they're equally bold. They've been known to tackle crocodiles up to 1m (3.28ft) long, and will even steal food from lions.

Ratels are also accomplished diggers and skilled climbers, and appear to have a natural immunity to venom, as shown in the 2002 National Geographic documentary, *Snake killers: honey badgers of the Kalahari*. In the film a ratel, called Kleinman, is seen to steal a meal out

Ratels are born opportunists and will eat almost anything, using their keen sense of smell to sniff out a meal.

Finding a burrow, our curious ratel blows down the entrance hole in an attempt to bring its owner into the open.

After several attempts to flush out his prey, he starts to dig – but there's still no sign of the burrow's occupant.

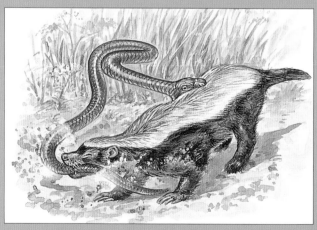

Success at last! The ratel gets his meal after all. Even an angry black mamba is no match for this hungry hunter.

Comparisons

Sunda stink badger

Ratel

Ratels and Sunda stink badgers *(Mydaus javanensis)* inhabit very different worlds. Ratels are the more successful of the two species, ranging from Africa to the Middle East and southern Asia. The Sunda stink badgers, which are smaller, are confined to the Indonesian islands of Java, Sumatra, North Natuna and Borneo. Both of these amiable-looking mammals are nocturnal hunters, emerging from their burrows just after dusk to feed.

of a puff adder's mouth before tackling the snake itself. After being bitten, the ratel collapsed but later recovered to continued eating!

Big and clever

What's in a name? In the case of the ratel, very little! Ratels are also known as honey badgers although they aren't badgers at all. Their closest relatives are skunks and, like all members of the Mustelidae family, ratels live up this group's smelly reputation. Scent marking is their main form of communication, and a male's daily patrol regularly takes him to the neighbourhood latrine. Here he'll mark his territory and check to see if any females in his range are ready to mate.

When it comes to the honey part of their name, though, these clever creatures really do have a surprisingly sweet tooth. Ratels are skilled hunters with a reputation for tackling some of nature's prickliest and most poisonous species. They are known to prey on at least 65 different animals, including scorpions, porcupines, young crocodiles and even venomous snakes, but honey is a firm favourite.

Ratels are big, powerful beasts, with razor-sharp claws and a hefty 14kg (30.9lb) bulk to throw behind any enterprise. If you happen to be a raiding bee hive, then it also helps to have a skin thick enough to deflect bee stings! However, the secret to the ratels' success is more about brains than brawn. Ratels have learnt – just like

Ratel habitats

people did – that, by following a bird known as a honeyguide, they'll always find a well-stocked hive. (And the bird gets to enjoy the honey once the ratel has had enough!) In fact, they are so smart that they're one of the few mammals recognized as 'tool users', often employing logs, twigs or rocks in surprisingly inventive ways to help to them access a tasty treat.

Siamese Fighting Fish

The brilliant colours and flowing fins of the Siamese fighting fish make them one of the most appealing aquarium species. Just don't be tempted to put these belligerent 'bettas' in a tank with anything else. Their reputation as fighting fish is well deserved!

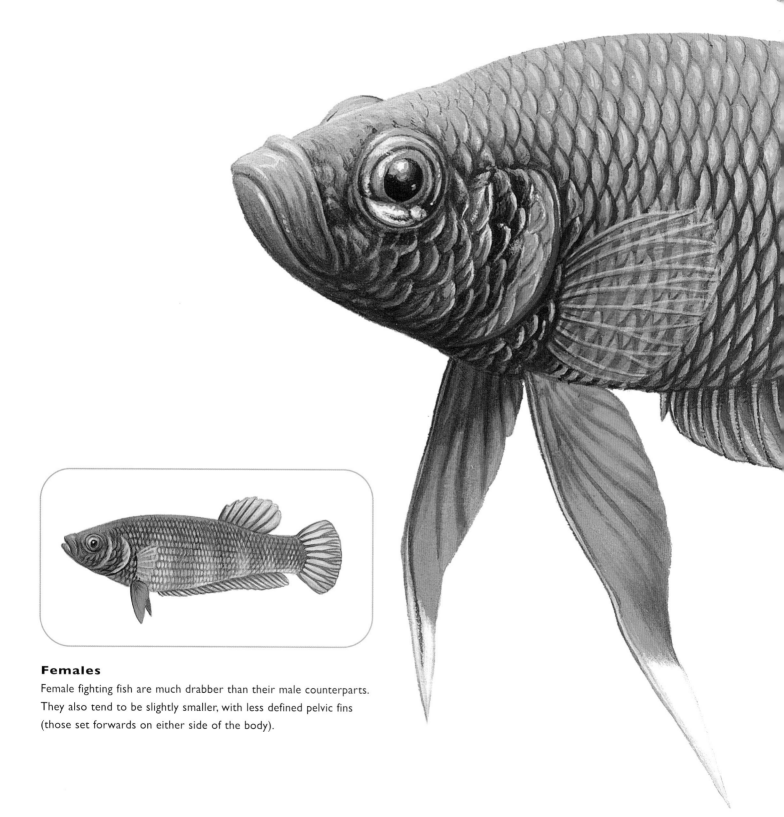

Females

Female fighting fish are much drabber than their male counterparts. They also tend to be slightly smaller, with less defined pelvic fins (those set forwards on either side of the body).

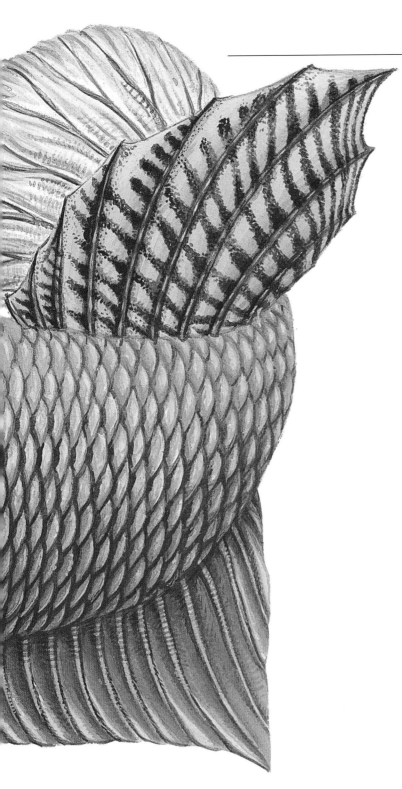

Key Facts

ORDER *Perciformes* / FAMILY *Belontiidae* / GENUS & SPECIES *Betta splendens*

Weight	Less than 10g (0.3oz)
Length	Up to 6cm (2.4in)
Sexual maturity	3–4 months
Breeding season	Not recorded
Number of eggs	Up to 500
Incubation period	24–30 hours
Breeding interval	Not recorded
Typical diet	Insects and insect larvae
Lifespan	Up to 2 years in the wild; 7 in captivity

Labyrinth organ

Inside the fighting fish's gill cavity is the labyrinth organ. This additional respiratory organ enables the fish to take oxygen directly from the air, rather than from the water.

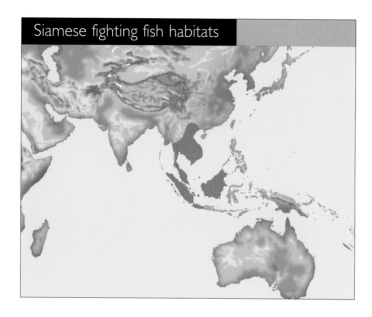

Siamese fighting fish habitats

There's nothing male Siamese fighting fish (also known as 'bettas') love more than a good ruckus! These beautifully iridescent fish may be small, but they're fiercely territorial and fights between rival males can be very bloody affairs.

In nature, it's usually the job of the male to attract a mate and, in order to do so, he must prove his prowess. Ritual displays are part of that process. Typically, these are highly stylized combats that rarely end in injury. The aim is to frighten off a rival rather than to wound or kill him, and threats and intimidation usually do the trick. Siamese fighting fish are unusual in that males and females are both extremely combative. Females often display to other females to establish their status and determine who is top

fish – but it's the males who are the real brawlers. They are so aggressive that, in captivity, two males can't be kept in the same tank. They will also attack other species of fish and will even try to fight their own reflections. In fact, they exhibit stress symptoms when these mirror intruders can't be chased away!

If a male fighting fish spots a rival straying into his territory, then it's all-out war. Combat begins with the usual display behaviour. The attacking male will rush at the intruder, fanning his fins and splaying out his gill covers to make himself look as big and as intimidating as possible. If threats fail, a flurry of attacks follow. The mouths of bettas are full of rows of tiny, pointed teeth, and rivals will bite each other's fins, jaws and bodies until one fish finally gives up and swims away to nurse his wounds.

Air and water
Naturally, Siamese fighting fish are found in a variety of habitats. They originate in Thailand (which was formerly called Siam, hence their name), and are also found in Indonesia, Malaysia, Vietnam and parts of China. They seem to prefer ponds and slow-moving streams, and their preference for shallow waters has made them popular pest controllers. They are often released into rice paddies, where they're happy in the shallows, gulping down insects and insect larvae.

Unlike most fish, fighting fish can tolerate waters that are choked with thick vegetation, and have a very low oxygen content. They are able to do this because they have an unusual extra organ. Within the fish world, there are some very strange and specialized species. There are fish that can

To prepare for mating, male fighting fish make a 'bubble nest' on the water's surface, using sticky, mucus-coated bubbles.

When the female is ready to spawn (lay her eggs), she approaches the nest, and an energetic courtship dance ensues.

walk. There are fish that can fly. But perhaps the most remarkable fish are those that breathe air.

Some fish breathe air using modified swim bladders. Others, like the lungfish, have developed rudimentary lungs. Fighting fish still have gills and use them to extract oxygen from the water, just like other fish. What sets this group apart from their relatives is the evocatively named labyrinth organ. This organ is formed from part of the gill arch and enables the fish to take oxygen directly from the air. The size of the organ varies depending on the environment in which each species lives. Sensibly, those that live in low-oxygen waters have larger and more complex labyrinth organs than species that make their homes in oxygen-rich waters. Regardless of the size of the organ, though, studies have shown that these labyrinth fish (belonging to the suborder *Anabantoidei*) rely on it to such an extent they they'd suffocate if it was removed.

Comparisons

Fighting fish are popular pets and fish fanciers have spent decades selectively breeding them to emphasize 'desired' traits and eliminate less desirable ones. The veiltail fighting fish is one of the most popular, aquarium-bred forms. These fish are bigger than wild fighting fish and have massively enlarged fins. They also tend to be just one colour, rather than multi-hued like their Siamese cousins.

Veiltail fighting fish

The male fertilizes the eggs, then corrals them into the waiting nest. For the next two days, he'll patiently stand guard.

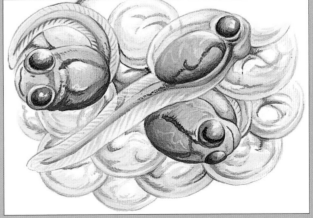

Once the young fry hatch, it takes only a few more days before they're strong enough to set off on their own.

Tarsier

You may have heard the expression 'your eyes are bigger than your belly', meaning to take more food than you can eat. But the eyes of tarsiers really are bigger than their bellies – and their brains! In fact, the tarsier is one very peculiar primate.

Key Facts	ORDER *Primates* / FAMILY *Tarsiidae* / GENUS & SPECIES *Genus tarsius*	
Weight	80–160g (2.8–5.6oz)
Length	Head and body: 8.5–16cm (3.3–6.3in) Tail: 13–27cm (5.1–10.6in)
Sexual maturity	15–18 months
Breeding season	All year
Number of young	1
Gestation period	6 months
Breeding interval	Twice a year
Typical diet	Insects and small vertebrates
Lifespan	Up to 12 years in the wild

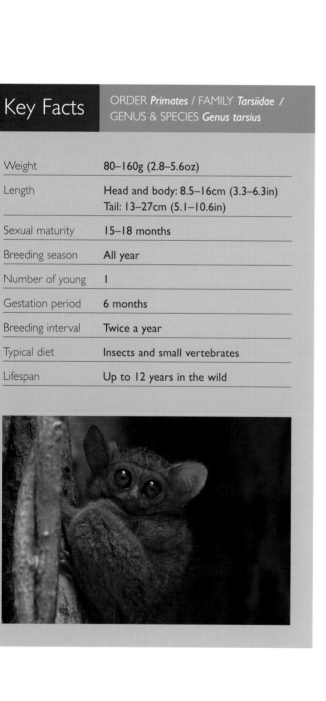

Teeth

Tarsiers are the only truly carnivorous primate. Sharp, stabbing teeth and broad crushing molars tell us that they have a varied diet – from insects to birds, to poisonous snakes.

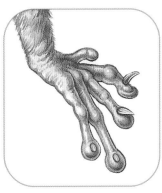

Toes

Long, slender fingers and toes tipped with fleshy pads help the tarsiers to grip on to both branches and prey. On the second and third toes are grooming claws.

Deep in the forests of south-east Asia live the descendants of an ancient line of primates, which can be traced back, through the fossil record, to the Eocene epoch, some 55.8–33.9 million years ago. This makes them unique. No other primate can be traced so clearly back to their ancient origins – and the tarsier seems to have changed little during this time.

Tarsiers are extremely shy creatures, and active mainly at night, which means that they spend the daytime holed up in tree cavities or hiding amongst lush vegetation. Their favourite place to be is asleep, upright, against a tree trunk or branch, using their tail for support. Naturally they're found in dense thickets of bamboo, rainforests and plantations, which makes them even harder to spot amongst the thick foliage. Yet, if we were lucky enough to see one of these rare and beautiful animals, we'd immediately notice how perfectly their bodies have developed to make the best of their environment.

Their hands and feet, for instance, are long and dextrous, with the added advantage of fleshy pads on the tips of their fingers and toes to give a better grip on branches. Their hind legs are also extremely long and designed for bounding from branch to branch. Their leaping abilities are legendary and on average they can cover 2m (6.6ft) with a single bound. During the course of these impressive acrobatics, they twist their bodies in the air and extend their fingers, ready to grasp the nearest branch. This peculiar mode of locomotion is aided by the tarsiers' elongated ankle bones, which work just like shock absorbers, to prevent injuries as they flit through the

These lithe tree-dwellers spend much of the day curled up asleep on a convenient branch, waking at dusk to hunt.

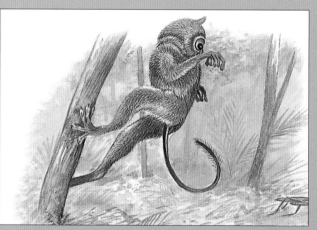

Using a branch as a launching pad, this tarsier makes good use of the element of surprise, to leap down on a passing cricket.

His intended victim makes a swift getaway but, undeterred, the tarsier gives chase – hopping across the ground with froglike leaps.

Success! Unfortunately, such an energetic pursuit of prey requires tarsiers to eat 10 per cent of their body weight in insects every night!

Comparisons

Senegal bush babies *(Galago senegalensis)* share many physical characteristics with Asian tarsiers. Like many night-time specialists, they have large eyes and, being an arboreal species, they have gripping hands and a long tail for balance. Bush babies are, however, the more social of the two. While some tarsier species prefer simply to pair up, bush baby females live in close knit groups with their young.

Tarsier

Senegal bush baby

forest. Indeed, the name tarsier refers to their enlarged tarsus (ankle) bone.

Wide-eyed and wonderful

No discussion about these wonderful creatures would be complete without reference to their most obvious and dramatic feature – their eyes. Tarsiers have huge eyes, each of which measures about 1.6cm (0.6in) in diameter.

Tarsier habitats

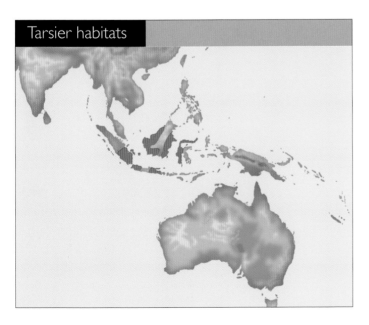

Amongst mammals, they have the largest eyes, in proportion to body size. In volume, the capacity of the tarsiers' eye sockets is larger than that of their brain case or their stomach.

Big eyes are important for nocturnal animals, as they help to collect as much light from the surrounding area as possible. However, tarsiers' eyes are not merely massive; they are also, structurally, quite strange. Many night-time specialists, especially hunters, have a region in the eye called the tapetum lucidum. This lies behind or sometimes within the retina and its job is to reflect visible light back through the retina. This helps to improve vision in low-light conditions. It's the tapetum lucidum that makes cats' eyes appear to glow in the dark. Tarsiers don't have a tapetum lucidum, but they do have a fovea – a very unusual feature for nocturnal animals. The fovea helps to sharpen images. In humans, it's the part of the eye which allows us to focus on the words on this page. So it's likely that these cute primates have extremely sharp, clear vision.

There's one further, odd thing about the tarsiers' odd eyes. They face forwards and can't move in the socket. Ordinarily, this would make it difficult for the tarsier to look out for prey or predators. Fortunately, over many millennia, these amazing animals have developed another unique ability to compensate. They have can rotate their head through almost 180° in both directions, a little like an owl.

PHILIPPINES

INDONESIA

PAPUA NEW
GUINEA

AUSTRALIA

Simpson
Desert

Great Victoria
Desert

Tasmania

SOUTH PACIFIC
OCEAN

SOUTHERN
OCEAN

NEW
ZEALAND

Australasia

If we could step back through history, instead of seeing the continents that are so familiar today, we'd find one vast landmass called Pangaea. This 'super continent' began to divide about 175 million years ago.

~

The breakup was a slow, almost imperceptible process – and one that took place while dinosaurs still walked the Earth. By the time of the Early Cretaceous period (some 146–100 million years ago), sections of Pangaea had begun to drift south. This movement would eventually create Australia, New Zealand and their surrounding islands.

Today, these spectacular island nations are often referred to as Australasia – a group that comprises Australia, New Zealand and their neighbours. The island of New Guinea, including Papua New Guinea, is also sometimes included as part of Australasia because it shares many economic and historic ties.

Humans found their way to the largest of these land masses, Australia, only about 48,000 years ago. New Zealand took much longer to be discovered. The first Polynesian migrants arrived there just 2000 years ago. And the rest of the world remained ignorant of the beauty of these great southern lands until European settlers come in the 1700s. And when they did come, they were amazed by what they found.

These spectacular islands had been isolated for so long that their flora and fauna were unlike anything that the settlers had ever seen before. Here was the emu, a giant bird that is unable to fly. Here was the echidna, a species that once lived alongside dinosaurs – and which has barely changed since. Here too was the duck-billed platypus, an animal so odd that European scientists could not believe it was real. And there were also kangaroos and koala bears. Welcome to Australasia!

Duck-billed Platypus

The duckbill platypus is probably one of Australia's oddest, native species. When British scientists first saw a specimen of this amazing creature, with its beaver-like tail, duck bill, flippers and fur, they believed that it was just an elaborate fake.

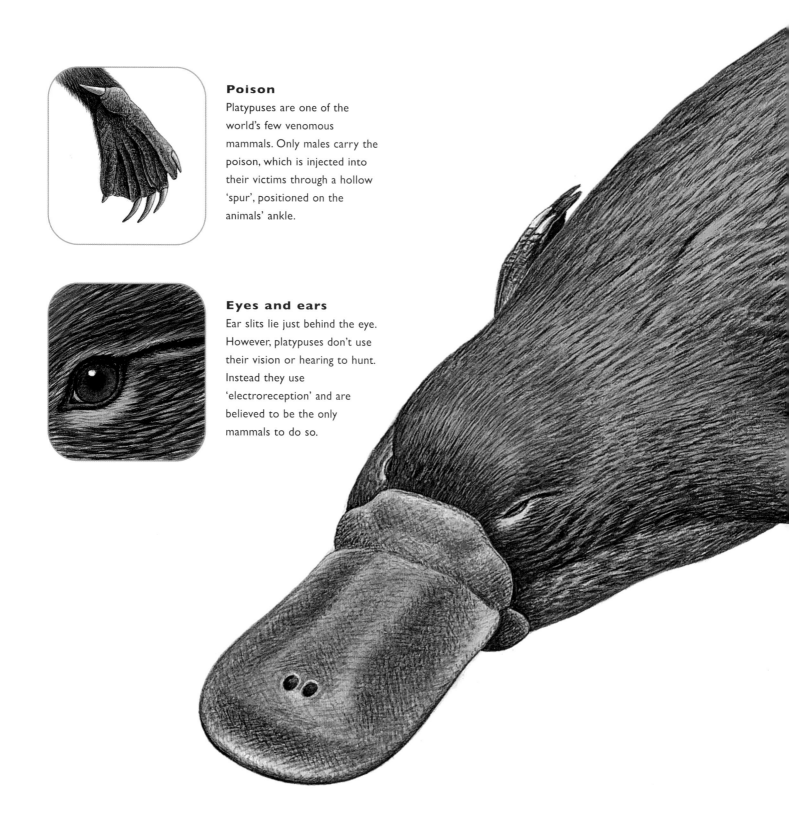

Poison

Platypuses are one of the world's few venomous mammals. Only males carry the poison, which is injected into their victims through a hollow 'spur', positioned on the animals' ankle.

Eyes and ears

Ear slits lie just behind the eye. However, platypuses don't use their vision or hearing to hunt. Instead they use 'electroreception' and are believed to be the only mammals to do so.

Key Facts

	ORDER *Monotremata* / FAMILY *Ornithorhyncidae* / GENUS & SPECIES *Ornithorhynchus anatinus*
Weight	0.7–2.4kg (1.5–5.3lb)
Length	Males: average 50cm (19.7in) Females: average 47 cm (18.5)
Sexual maturity	2 years
Breeding season	June–October but varies across range
Number of eggs	1–3
Incubation period	10 days
Breeding interval	1–2 years
Typical diet	Insect larvae, fish and amphibians
Lifespan	Up to 11 years in the wild; 17 in captivity

Duck-billed platypus habitats

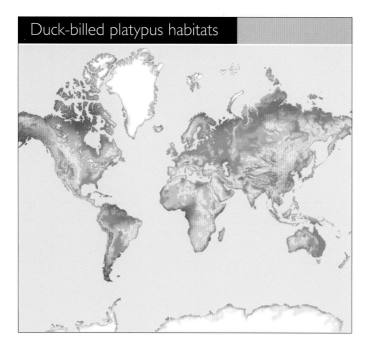

The first British settlers in Australia weren't sure what to make of the platypus. Calling it 'duckmole', they were so puzzled they sent the pelt from a juvenile male to Britain for examination. There, the first scientists to look at it, in 1798, thought that it had been made up. The Scottish anatomist Robert Knox (1791–1862) described it as a 'freak imposture' while the zoologist George Shaw (1751–1813) went so far as checking the skin for stitches, believing that it had been faked by a taxidermist. You can still see the scissor marks that he made on the pelt to this day! Once these marvellous mammals have been seen in

the flesh, however, it becomes clear just how strange they really are.

Although platypus numbers have fallen in recent years, populations can still be found in eastern Australia and Tasmania. They prefer river areas with muddy banks and overhanging vegetation, and it's here that they make their homes. Platypuses have short legs, webbed fore feet and partially webbed hind feet. In the water, their fore feet move with alternate strokes, using a rowing motion to propel them forwards. (Their hind feet and tail do the steering.) On land, these feet are 'turned back', uncovering their claws, which can be used to dig.

Platypuses are shy, solitary creatures and, apart from when females nurse their young, each has their own, private burrow. Those used by males are generally quite short but 'nursery burrows' can be up to 18m (59ft) long with a nest of leaves and grass at the end. Before laying her eggs, a female platypus will block the entrance to her burrow with earth to protect against floodwaters and predators and ensure the safety of her new family.

Eggs-traordinary!

Platypus eggs develop in utero (inside the uterus) for about 28 days before they are laid. The platypus lays one to three eggs (typically two), which have parchment-like shells resembling reptile eggs. It takes a further 10 days for the eggs to hatch and, during this time, the mother will curl herself round them to ensure that they remain at a constant temperature – never too hot or too cold.

What's so surprising about this process is that platypuses are mammals. The only other mammal group that lays eggs

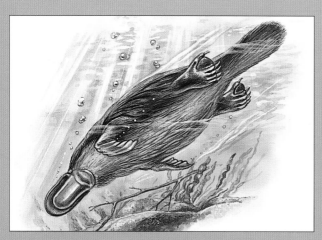

Diving deep, the predatory platypus propels itself through the water using its front legs only. Hind legs and tail steer.

As it searches for titbits on the river bed, it shuts its eyes and ears, using its bill to detect prey.

Comparisons

These wonderfully odd mammals belong to a group known as monotremes. Unlike most mammals and marsupials, monotremes lay eggs rather than give birth to live young. Membership of this elite clique is limited to just two groups – the platypuses and the echidnas. Although they share common ancestors, echidnas diverged from platypuses 19–48 million years ago, when they returned to a completely land-based life.

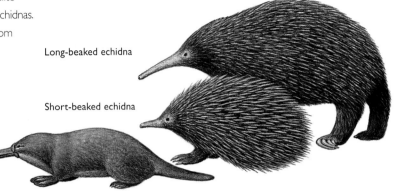

Long-beaked echidna

Short-beaked echidna

Duck-billed platypus

are the echidnas, which are monotremes like the platypus. Generally egg-laying is something that's associated with reptiles – although in this volume you'll find exceptions to that rule too! (See the entry for Jackson's chameleon on pages 26–29.)

So if platypuses lay eggs but are still classified as mammals, then what is it that makes a mammal a mammal? Reptiles are usually described as being cold-blooded 'vertebrates' (animals with backbones) whose bodies are covered in scales or bony plates. Mammals are typically defined as warm-blooded, air-breathing vertebrates. Mammals usually give birth to live young –

and feed them on milk from mammary glands, which is where the word mammal originates. So, although platypuses lay eggs, it's the fact that the females feed them on milk – produced by mammary glands – that makes them a mammal

Of course, because platypuses are intrinsically strange, there is one slight difference to the usual set-up. Platypuses don't have teats, so when the youngsters want to feed, they tap their mother on the flanks, which stimulates her to release milk through the pores in her skin. This milk collects in special grooves, ready to be lapped up by her hungry offspring.

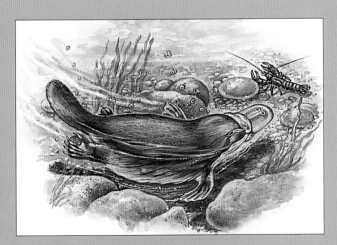

This bill is covered in sensitive receptors, which pick up the electric fields that are generated by muscle contractions.

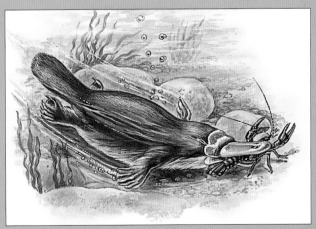

These receptors are so accurate that the platypus can find prey up to 10cm (3.9in) away.

Emu

Australia is famous for its strange creatures, but these giant, flightless birds are real curiosities. Looking like some shaggy over-grown turkey, emus are now frequently found on farms. But wild birds continue to surprise – and amuse – visitors to this unique continent.

Key Facts	ORDER *Casuariformes* / FAMILY *Dromaiidae* / GENUS & SPECIES *Dromaius novaehollandiae*
Weight	Up to 50kg (110.3lb)
Length	Up to 1.9m (6.2ft)
Sexual maturity	2 years
Breeding season	April–June
Number of eggs	Up to 20
Incubation period	56 days
Breeding interval	Females mate multiple times through year.
Typical diet	Seeds, shoots and insects
Lifespan	10–20 years in the wild

Feathers

Emu feathers have a unique structure. A second shaft, as long as the first, sprouts from the base of the main feather.

Male

Pale blue skin on the neck is visible through a sparse covering of feathers. This is lighter in males.

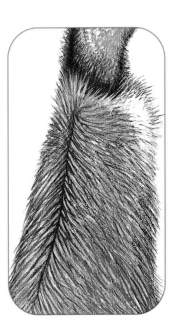

Parting

A distinct parting in the heavy, hairlike plumage of these huge birds runs down the neck and along the back.

Being big doesn't necessarily mean that you can't get airborne – it just makes it a lot harder! The extinct *Argentavis magnificens,* for instance, weighed up to 110kg (242.5lb). It was the largest bird that ever flew and needed massive flight muscles and an 8m (26.2ft) wingspan to get into the air. So, a bird the size of an emu would certainly be able to fly, if its body was designed to do so. Unfortunately, it isn't.

Flight is about more than just feathers and wings – it's dependent also on the design of the body – and most birds have a number of physical adaptations that aid flight. Their skeletons, for instance, are lightweight. They have fewer bones than other vertebrates and many of these are hollow. They have circulatory and respiratory systems that have to work at an incredibly high rate to power flight. They have wings that are specially shaped to reduce drag and increase lift. But it's the birds' sternum (breastbone) that is particularly important. This large bone lies beneath the body and, in those species that fly, it has an enormous, projecting keel, to which the flight muscles are attached. This keeled shape adds strength and enables the sternum to bear the stresses of flight.

Some flightless birds retain many physical features that tell us that their ancestors once flew. Some even have a keeled sternum, although their wings are too small, and their bodies too big, for them to get airborne. However, emus are members of a strange group of flightless birds called ratites, which have flat keels. So, even if their stubby wings were bigger and their shabby, hairlike plumage was

Emu habitats

replaced with finely preened flight feathers, they still wouldn't be able to fly.

Bird wars

In the past, birds like New Zealand's quirky kakapo *(Strigops habroptila)* didn't have to worry about getting airborne because the islands on which lived had no ground-dwelling predators. So, as time progressed, they lost the ability to fly. It was only when humans arrived in the

Comparisons

Emus may be Australia's biggest bird, but they're not the world's only big birds. South America has its own giants, known as greater rheas *(Rhea americana).* The biggest of these impressive birds weigh in at 40kg (88.2lb) and stand over 1.5m (4.9ft) tall. Like the 'antipodean' emus, they're flightless, with long, powerful legs and a long neck designed for foraging on the ground.

Greater rhea

Emu

Male emus are devoted parents. For eight weeks, they sit on the nest, while the female leaves the male to hold the baby.

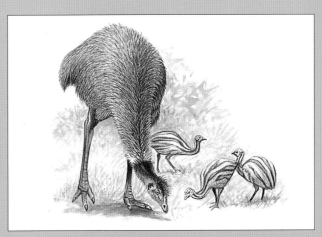

Once they've hatched, the father takes charge of the chicks – protecting them and teaching them how to forage for food.

While the chicks are happy to make friends, their father is wary of the approaching male and attempts to drive him away.

If the interloper stands his ground, things could get nasty! Emus don't pull their punches – or their kicks!

region, that everything changed. The giant moa *(Dinornis)* became the first victim of these new arrivals. These enormous ratites grew up to 3.6m (12ft) tall, but their great size offered them no protection from humans. Between the thirteenth and fourteenth centuries, these gentle giants were hunted to extinction. Later, European settlers continued the trend and brought with them other predators – rats and cats – against which flightless species had no defence.

Compared to Australasia's other flightless species, then, emus have come out of this clash between man and beast relatively unscathed. On the Australian mainland, these bizarre beasts have been hunted for their oil, meat, eggs and leather for as long as people have lived on the continent. In 1932, there was even an 'emu war', when the government sent out troops to cull the rising numbers of emus that were destroying farmers' crops. Yet these hardy and adaptable creatures have survived it all. In part this may be due to their speed. When trouble strikes, their powerful legs can carry them out of danger at speeds of 48km/h (30mph)!

Flocks of wild emu are no longer as widespread as they once were, but because these fabulous birds are nomadic – migrating with the rains – they always find food. And they can survive for weeks before they do. Their strange plumage insulates their skin and enables them to endure life even in Australia's baking hot plains. The only region they avoid are the deserts.

Koala

Like China's giant panda *(Ailuropoda melanoleuca)*, koalas occupy a unique 'ecological niche'. They have developed to live almost entirely on eucalypt leaves. Few other animals could survive on such toxic, low-calorie food, and even the koala barely subsists on such a poor diet!

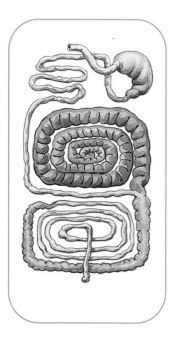

Caecum

Two metres (6.6ft) long, this area of the gut contains many of the bacteria needed for digesting such tough food.

Hands and Feet

Most primates have opposable thumbs, which are thumbs that can bend to touch all of the fingers. Koalas go one better. On each hand, they have two opposable thumbs – and each foot has an opposable thumb as well!

Key Facts	ORDER *Diprotondonta* / FAMILY *Phascolarctidae* / GENUS & SPECIES *phascolarctos cinereus*
Weight	Males: 12kg (26.4lb) Females: 8kg (17.6lb)
Length	63–80cm (24.8–31.5in)
Sexual maturity	Males: 3–4 years. Females: 2–3 years
Breeding season	December–January
Number of young	1
Gestation period	35 days
Breeding interval	Yearly
Typical diet	Eucalypt leaves
Lifespan	20 years in the wild

Baby koalas spend the first 24–28 weeks of life inside their mother's pouch, feeding on the milk she provides.

Koalas pouches open downwards, which enables the growing baby to take in additional food from a very unusual source.

They eat predigested food in the form of soft droppings! These contain the bacteria necessary to digest eucalypt leaves.

Once the baby has developed a tolerance to eucalypt leaves, it can begin to feed for itself. This happens at about seven months.

They're cute, cuddly and covered in soft fur, but, while these delightfully dozy animals may look like teddies, the name 'koala bear' is a real misnomer. Koalas aren't bears at all.

Bears belong to the scientific family group *Ursidae*, but koalas are part of the Phascolarctidae family. In fact, they're the only living member of this group. Koalas are also marsupials while bears are placental mammals. In mammals, the unborn young grow inside their mother's body, where they are supplied with nutrients and oxygen by an organ called a placenta. It's only once the young are fully formed that they're born. Marsupials take a different approach. Their young are born at an extremely immature stage of development, when they are tiny, blind and almost limbless. Development continues in the pouch, which can almost be considered as an external womb.

It used to be believed that marsupials were an earlier, less sophisticated type of mammal, but it's now thought that both branches of the mammal family tree developed independently at around same time, during the end of the Mesozoic era. The earliest known marsupial is *Sinodelphys szalayi,* which lived in China around 125 million years ago. This is the same age as the earliest known placental mammal. It also confirms the long-held assumption that marsupials originated in south-east Asia and, indeed, some still live in this region. However, the ancestors of today's Australian marsupials had an incredible journey to reach the continent. They began by heading west, into North

America, which was still attached to Eurasia at that point. From there, they headed to South America. They finally reached Australia via Antarctica about 50 million years ago, just after the two continents split.

Carving out a niche

This was a moment when rainforest covered much of the country, but as the climate changed, the rainforest was replaced by eucalypt forest. Koalas now live in the tall eucalypt forests of eastern Australia and on some islands off the southern and eastern coasts. These animals have been able to survive by adapting to eat what no other animal will – eucalypt leaves.

Occupying an environmental niche like this has great advantages. Koalas never have to fight with rivals for food, for instance. This is because compounds in the leaves are toxic to most species. Giant pandas have specialized in a similar way, but are facing extinction now because they rely on bamboo forests, which suffer from huge, natural 'die-offs' and are also being cut down by developers. Eucalypt is much better choice from a survival point of view, there are 680 species – of which blue gum, grey gum and red river gum seem to be the koalas' favourites.

The koalas' problem is that eucalypt leaves are so low in calories that they need to eat 500g (17.6oz) of leaves a day to survive. These need to be munched into a thick paste before they can be swallowed. It's then that the koalas' extra long gut comes into its own. This is needed to break down the tough leaves, remove their toxins and

Koala habitats

extract every ounce of food value. Koalas eat so much eucalypt foliage that it's been said that they share the leaves' distinctive odour, which is a little like cough drops!

However, even with such a big intake of food, these fluffy-eared mammals still have to spend 18 hours asleep to conserve energy! Koalas have such a low metabolic rate that if you're lucky enough to see one it will most likely be tucked in the nook of a tree, or wedged between two forked branches, fast asleep.

Comparisons

There are three living species of wombat, and these cute but tough marsupials can be found in many of the same areas as their koala cousins. Both animal groups have an amazingly slow metabolism, which helps them survive in extreme conditions. But, while koalas prefer an arboreal life, the chubby-cheeked wombats are subterranean and use their rodent-like teeth and sharp claws to dig burrows.

Koala

Wombat

Laughing Kookaburra

Laughing kookaburras are members of the well-known and dramatically colourful kingfisher family (order *Coraciiformes*). These handsome birds make their homes all over the Old World of Africa, Asia and Europe but, like many of Australia's native species, the Antipodean kookaburras are real ornithological oddities.

Key Facts

ORDER *Coraciiformes* / FAMILY *Alcadinidae* / GENUS & SPECIES *Dacelo novaeguineae*

Weight	368–455g (13–16.1oz)
Length	39–45cm (15.3–17.7in)
Sexual maturity	1 year
Breeding season	October–November
Number of eggs	3, but second clutch is possible
Incubation period	25–29 days
Breeding interval	Yearly
Typical diet	Small rodents and reptiles
Lifespan	Up to 11 years in the wild; 20 in captivity.

Bill
A stocky bill can grow to 10cm (3.9in) long. A hook on the tip helps grip struggling prey.

Tail
A relatively short tail is rusty red with dark brown bars and splashes of white on the tips of the feathers.

Foot

For such large birds,
kookaburras have
surprisingly small, weak feet.
Three toes face forwards
and one faces backwards.

The laughing kookaburra takes its name from its disinctive and unusual call: *koo-koo-koo-kaa-kaa-KAA!-KAA!-KAA!!* Interestingly, these birds tend to call out in unison rather than singly.

Generally one bird begins the distinctive call, with a low, choked chuckle, before throwing its head back in a fit of uncontrolled laughter. Other members of the group quickly add their own voices to the rising chorus, to create a raucous row. This amazing 'alarm call' is usually heard just after after dawn or dusk, which is why the laughing kookaburra is also known by another, equally evocative nickname – the Bushman's Clock.

The reason that these beautiful birds create such a kerfuffle is to establish and maintain their territorial claims.

They live in family groups, and the fledglings from one breeding season often stay in the family group, helping to raise the next generation of chicks. So, in effect, what the kookaburra families are saying is: 'Here we are' and 'We're big and loud, and you don't want to mess with us'. If a rival family group is within earshot, they'll usually reply, until the whole area is ringing with hoots of hysterical laughter. It is a sound that cannot be ignored – and can be inimidating to those who aren't expecting it.

The call of the laughing kookaburra is such a famous feature of the Australian bush that it's been immortalized in a popular children's song: 'Kookaburra sits in the old gum tree, Merry merry king of the woods is he! Laugh Kookaburra, Laugh Kookaburra! How gay your life must

Kookaburras are patient, highly skilled ambush-hunters. They are kingfishers but, unlike their European relatives, they hunt over land not water.

A snake makes a tasty titbit and kookaburras have a special technique for dealing with such slippery – and potentially poisonous – prey.

By thrashing the snake, repeatedly, against the hard earth, the kookaburra quickly stuns, and eventually kills, its writhing midday meal.

Now the kookaburra is free to eat without fear of being bitten. This serpentine snack goes down very well – and whole!

Laughing kookaburra habitats

woodlands and scrub, where they spend their days perched, in the shade, waiting to swoop down on some unsuspecting victim. Small mammals, reptiles and insects are their preferred choices, but they will attack larger creatures. They even catch snakes. They're just as fast and agile in the air as their smaller counterparts but − although they do occasionally pinch ornamental fish from garden ponds − they hunt on land, rather than water.

Like many hunters, they'll take easy pickings. They will accept food offered to them by people. And food prepared for a barbecue is an easy steal − they'll even dare to take it from the hot grill.

be!' And the bird itself was one of the mascots for the Sydney Olympics in 2000.

Curious kingfishers

For many years, these appealing birds were known as 'laughing jackasses' or 'giant kingfishers'. They're now much more commonly referred to by their Aboriginal name − the kookaburra.

These elegantly proportioned hunters belong to the kingfisher family *Halcyonidae*, which includes about 61 species. In common with most members of this family, laughing kookaburras have a distinctive shape. Their bodies are relatively compact, with a large head and truncated tail. Wings are short and bills are long and sharp, although kookaburras have a much broader bill than the usual dagger-like kingfisher design. Their plumage is also quite plain, with none of the shimmering greens, blues and oranges that many other species favour.

What they lack in dress sense, however, they more than make up for in physical presence. Laughing kookaburras are the largest species of kingfisher and are, proportionately, bulkier and heavier then river or tree kingfishers. Compared to the laughing kookaburra, the common kingfisher *(Alcedo atthis)* is almost three times smaller, with a body length of just 16cm (6.3in).

Species like *Alcedo atthis* are famously skilled hunters. Thanks to their streamlined shape. they are able to dive into water and pluck fish from their own element with relative ease. It's because of this behaviour that they were given the descriptive epithet, 'king fishers'. Kookaburras, though, are 'generalists'. They make their homes in

Comparisons

The iridescent plumage of the blue-winged kookaburra *(Dacelo leachii)* brings to mind the dramatic rainbow-hued common kingfisher *(Alcedo atthis)*, which is so popular throughout Eurasia. In comparison, the laughing kookaburra seems like the poor relation of the family − with its 'work-a-day' brown and white plumage. Yet, in the flesh, both birds are undeniably impressive. The blue-winged kookaburras are more widespread, but in eastern Australia their ranges overlap.

Blue-winged kookaburra

Laughing kookaburra

Red Kangaroo

Everything about the red kangaroo is big. They're the largest living marsupial, the largest Australian mammal and they have the ability to jump 25ft (8m) in a single bound. When it comes to the kangaroo's young, though, these big mammals produce tiny, bean-sized joeys.

Teeth

Four pairs of cheek teeth sit on either side of the jaws. As the front ones wear down, they fall out. Those at the back then move forwards to take their place.

Pouch

A muscular 'band' keeps the pouch tightly closed. This not only prevents the joey from falling out when its mother is on the move, but ensures a constant, temperature of 32°C (90°F).

Key Facts

	ORDER *Marsupialia* / FAMILY *Macropodidae* / GENUS & SPECIES *Macropus rufus*
Weight	Up to 90kg (198.4lb)
Length	Up to 1.6m (5.2ft) Tail: up to 1.1m (3.6ft)
Sexual maturity	15–24 months
Breeding season	All year
Number of young	1
Gestation period	5–6 months
Breeding interval	Females become fertile every 35 days if not suckling young
Typical diet	Grasses and flowering plants
Lifespan	Up to 22 years in the wild; 16 years in captivity

Red kangaroo habitats

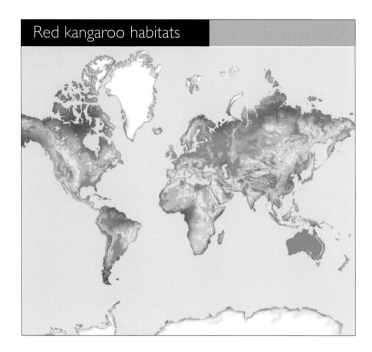

For a kangaroo, walking is quite a tricky process. To do so, 'roos must swing their huge, hind legs forwards, while supporting their body on their short arms and powerful tail. It's an ungainly method of getting about and belies the fact that, at speed, these great Australian animals are truly awesome. Then, they bound, like some impossibly giant rabbit, with their hind legs propelling them forwards, and their tails held almost horizontally as a counterweight. A

male kangaroo can jump up to 9m (30ft) in one leap. So, though this is a strange method of locomotion, it lets kangaroos reach speeds of over 56km/h (35mph). Even 'cruising speed' is an impressive 20-25km/h (13-16mph).

They can reach such staggering speeds due to the combination of powerful legs and long, hind feet. On each hind foot is an enlarged fourth toe. This is lined up with the kangaroo's leg bone which, in turn, is anchored by 'elastic' tendons more than 1cm (0.4in) thick. When 'roos hop, both hind feet hit the ground simultaneously. The effect is like someone pushing down on a huge spring. Relax, and the tension is released and the kangaroo 'ricochets' forwards.

But why hop rather than walk? There's some evidence that kangaroos didn't always move around in such a dramatic fashion. Fossils seem to show that it was the development of their over-sized fourth toe that gave them the ability to bound. Once this happened, 'roos never looked back. Although it may look like an extremely tiring way to get around, hopping is very efficient: the faster they move, the more efficiently their bodies work. In fact, modern-day kangaroos have no choice but to hop because, except when they swim, their hind legs can't move independently.

Beanie babies
It took almost 300 years for scientists to discover exactly how baby kangaroos are born and reach the pouch. Even

Comparisons

Throughout the Australian continent, kangaroos and their marsupial cousins have adapted to fill a range of environmental niches. Larger species, like the red kangaroo, are creatures of the open, grassy plains. The medium-sized pademelons (genus Thylogale) enjoy life in and around thick scrubland and dense forests. And boodies (Bettongia lesueur), which are small, ratlike marsupials, make their homes in open, sandy regions – perfect for burrowing.

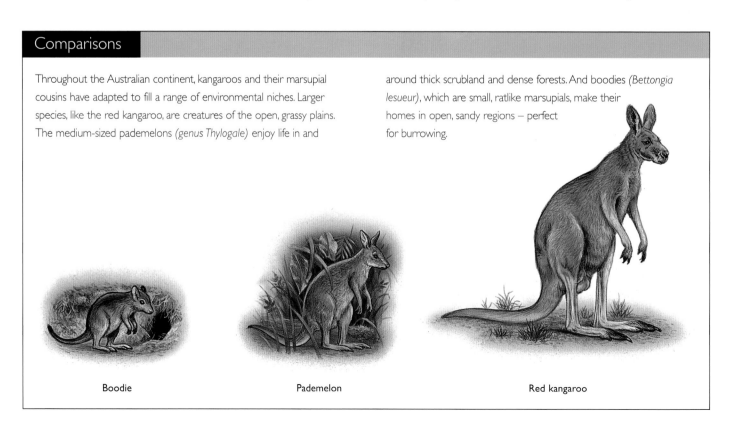

Boodie

Pademelon

Red kangaroo

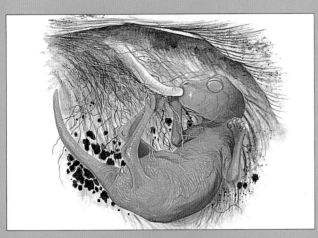

Once the tiny embryonic kangaroo reaches its mother's pouch, it attaches itself to a teat and begins to feed.

Here he'll stay, until he's big enough to fend for himself, by which time, the pouch is quite a tight fit!

Regular feeds keep the joey fit and healthy. By now, a brother or sister may be on the way too.

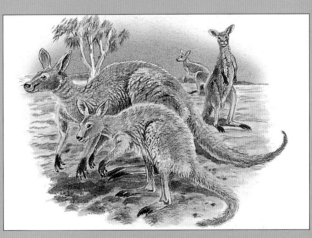

By the time he's aged 1, the joey no longer needs his mother's milk, but he'll stay by her side until he's sexually mature.

once the process had been observed, it wasn't until this was filmed, in 1959, that people really believed it!

It was in 1629 that a Dutch sea Caption, Francois Pelsaert, first reported seeing a baby joey in the pouch of a wallaby (a relative of the kangaroo). Native people believed that the babies were born in the pouch and this is what the Captain reported, and what was accepted as fact until 1830. Then, Alexander Collie, an amateur naturalist, managed to observe a joey being born – and it happened in the usual mammalian way – down the birth canal.

Joeys are born at a much earlier stage of physical development than is usual. Even in red kangaroos, which are the largest species, the baby emerges after just 33 days in the womb. At this point, they're little more than bean-sized embryos – blind, hairless and only a few centimetres long. So no one knew exactly how this tiny creature could possibly make its way from the birth canal to the pouch. Several suggestions were put forwards, but it was only in 1913 that a tiny neonate was actually observed, using its fore arms to haul itself through its mother's fur and into the pouch. This seemed like such an incredible feat that no one could really believe it. Even when it was confirmed by the Director of New York's Zoological Gardens in 1923, many people were were still unconvinced. Finally, the whole process was caught on film and the world was, at last, able to marvel at the momentous achievement of these bean-sized babies.

Short-beaked Echidna

These extraordinary, egg-laying mammals make their homes throughout
Australia and New Guinea. Despite their comical, waddling gait and wire-brush
bodies, these distinctive 'spiny anteaters' are true survivors. They have been so
successful as a species that they've changed little since their ancestors walked
with dinosaurs.

Key Facts	ORDER *Monotremata* / FAMILY *Tachyglossidae* / GENUS & SPECIES *Tachyglossus aculeatus*
Weight	2–7kg (4.4–15.4lb) depending on subspecies
Length	30–45cm (11.8–17.7in) depending on subspecies
Sexual maturity	4–5 years
Breeding season	May–Sept but varies throughout range
Number of eggs	1
Incubation period	21–28 days
Breeding interval	2–6 years
Typical diet	Ants and termites
Lifespan	Up to 45 years in the wild; 50 in captivity

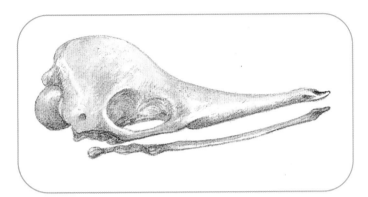

Skull
Echidnas' skulls are shaped for specialist feeding. A small head is tipped with a birdlike 'beak', with which they sniff out food.

Feet
Echidna are powerful diggers. Both sexes have long claws, which they use to dig out prey and make burrows. Males have an extra 'spur' on their hind feet, but unlike in platypuses, these do not carry poison.

Comparisons

Prickly 'hair' makes great defensive armour and the short-beaked echidna is only one of several mammals that has evolved such specialized spines. Echidna are found throughout Australasia, but they have their counterparts in the Northern Hemisphere too. Hedgehogs may be smaller than the echidna, but both have similar ways of dealing with unwanted guests. They curl their bodies into a ball, exposing only their spines to attackers.

Hedgehog

Short-beaked echidna

Short-beaked echidna habitats

From tropical rainforests to the dry Australian outback, from meadows to the clogged city suburbs, echidna are able to make themselves at home almost anywhere. There are five subspecies of short-beaked echidna. Australia, New Guinea, Tasmania and Kangaroo Island all boast their own 'native' subspecies - each perfectly adapted to suit their particular environment. In fact, although New Guinea's *Tachyglossus aculeatus lawesii* is struggling to adapt to habitat loss, echidna are coping better than many species with the stresses and strains of the modern world.

With their elongated snouts, short legs, rotund bodies and characteristic spines, these marvellous mammals may look strange, but they're designed to thrive and survive in the harshest of conditions.

Although their spines are their most notable feature, echidnas also have a coat of short, coarse fur to protect them from cold. Those subspecies living in Tasmania have longer, thicker fur than those living in warmers areas. When the cold really begins to bite, though, they simply hunker down in their burrow and go to sleep. Echidna can slow down their metabolisms to save energy, entering a hibernation-like state when the weather is bad and food is scarce. It wasn't until 2007 that this behaviour was observed by Professor Gordon Grigg, who was then Zoology Professor at the University of Queensland. He discovered echidnas hibernating above the snow line of Australia's highest mountain, Mount Kosciuszko, which is 2228m (7310ft) above sea level!

Luckily, most echidna don't need to hibernate because Australia has an abundance of their favourite foods. Termites, worms and insect larvae are all eagerly munched down by hungry echidna, but the species are keen formicivores – they particularly love ants. So anywhere there are ants, there will probably also be echidnas.

Amazing monotremes

There's more to this species than meets the eye. It may have changed little since the time of the dinosaurs, but they're far from primitive. Echidnas belong to a group of animals known as monotremes. Unlike most mammals and marsupials, monotremes lay eggs rather than give birth to live young. Membership of this elite clique is limited to just the platypuses and the echidnas. Although both share common ancestors, the echidna branch of the family diverged 19–48 million years ago and, in the process, developed some quite surprising and sophisticated characteristics.

For instance, echidnas have no teeth. They don't need them! Their short limbs and powerful front claws are perfect for digging and tearing open rotting logs, termite mounds and ant hills. Once inside, echidna need only lap up the contents with speedy flicks of their tongue. Tiny spines on the tongue help to catch the insects, and when the tongue is retracted, these are caught on backwards-facing 'plates' that sit on the roof of the mouth. These

plates are made from keratin – the same material as in human fingernails – and they are tough enough to grind up even the biggest, crunchiest termite with ease!

The echidnas' leathery snout is covered in sensitive receptors, which provide them with information about their surrounding environment. They have an extremely well-developed sense of smell and excellent vision. They have bigger brains than similar-sized creatures along with a highly developed cerebral cortex. This is the area of the brain responsible for attention, perception and memory. Studies have shown that echidnas have superb memories and excellent spatial awareness. So it seems to be no fluke that this ancient line of mammals has managed to survive the pressures of life in the twenty-first century.

Echidnas are solitary – until the breeding season, when females leave enticing scent-messages for potential mates.

Interested males pick up the scent and a bizarre race begins as they track her every move, jostling to get close to her.

After up to four weeks of tireless pursuit, the female digs a safe hidey hole and leaves the frenzied males to fight it out.

To the victor come the spoils of war! Usually the biggest male wins the day and the chance to mate.

Sugar Glider

Marsupials – those mammals that carry their undeveloped young in pouches – have been surprising scientists since the 1700s. Including kangaroos and koalas, marsupials each have their share of curious characteristics, but sugar gliders can even take to the air!

Mouth

Sharp incisor teeth enable sugar gliders to gouge holes in tree bark. They then lap up the sugary sap.

Feet

Opposable thumbs and four long fingers on both hands and feet give sugar gliders an excellent grip when climbing.

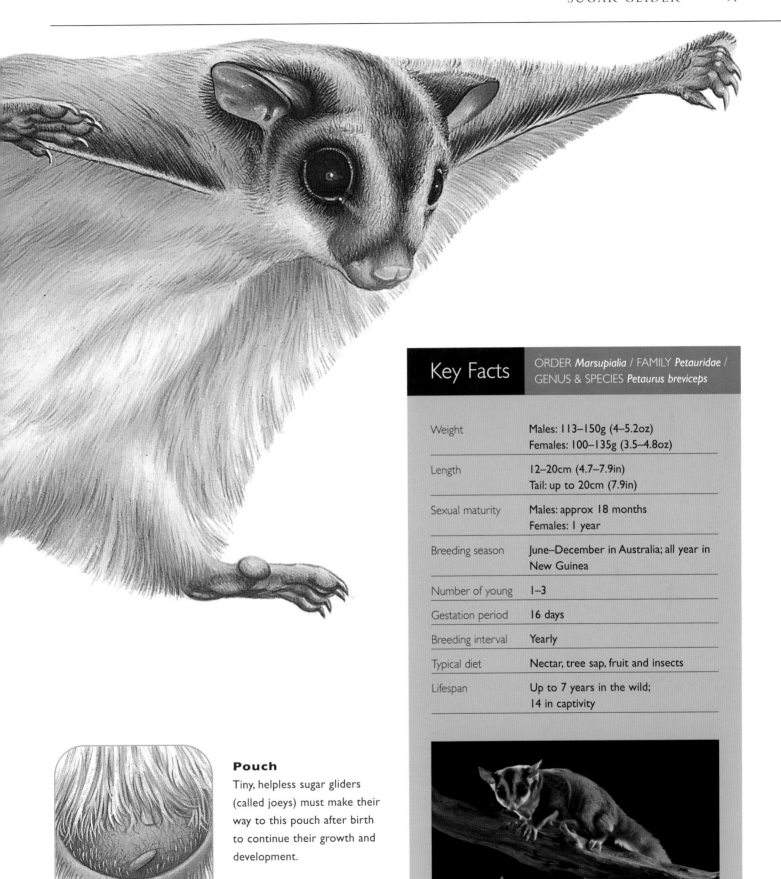

Key Facts

	ORDER *Marsupialia* / FAMILY *Petauridae* / GENUS & SPECIES *Petaurus breviceps*
Weight	Males: 113–150g (4–5.2oz) Females: 100–135g (3.5–4.8oz)
Length	12–20cm (4.7–7.9in) Tail: up to 20cm (7.9in)
Sexual maturity	Males: approx 18 months Females: 1 year
Breeding season	June–December in Australia; all year in New Guinea
Number of young	1–3
Gestation period	16 days
Breeding interval	Yearly
Typical diet	Nectar, tree sap, fruit and insects
Lifespan	Up to 7 years in the wild; 14 in captivity

Pouch

Tiny, helpless sugar gliders (called joeys) must make their way to this pouch after birth to continue their growth and development.

Launching itself from a handy branch, the sugar glider spreads out its arms and legs to reveal a 'gliding membrane'.

By adjusting the tightness of the membrane and the angle of its tail, the sugar glider is able to 'steer' through the forest.

There are exceptions to every rule. Not every bird can fly, and not every mammal is earthbound. Bats are the only true fliers in the mammal kingdom, but that doesn't mean they're the only mammals to take to the air. Squirrels, possums and colugos are all accomplished gliders. Fish, squid, lizards and snakes have mastered the art, too!

According to a new fossil, found in China in 2006, mammals probably took to the skies during the Mesozoic era. That's around 70 million years earlier than was initially thought and around the same time as birds were trying to develop the ability to fly. It's believed that this ancient, squirrel-sized mammal, dubbed *Volaticotherium antiquum*

Sugar glider habitats

(meaning 'ancient gliding beast'), used a fur-covered membrane to sweep through the air in much the same way as today's gliders do.

Unlike flight, which is powered, controlled movement, gliding relies on gravity. So sugar gliders usually start from a high perch and then drift downwards to a lower perch. It's not an exact science, and in some species it can be little more than controlled falling! Yet, as David Attenborough demonstrated in his BBC TV documentary *The Life of Mammals,* some gliders, like the colugo, can control the direction of their fall. Sugar gliders seem to be highly skilled too. They can glide distances of up to 45m (147.6ft) and even catch moths in flight.

Gliding may seem inefficient compared to flying, but it offers great advantages to those species that master it. It enables them to cover great distances relatively quickly. It offers a quick get-away route when danger threatens and, in the case of sugar gliders, it carries them from one meal of tree sap to another with little effort.

Amazing marsupials

It was the Swedish botanist Carl Linnaeus (1707–78) who first developed a usable system of scientific nomlecature to describe and classify animals. This placed all animals in distinct categories, which are determined by shared physical characteristics. His basic principles are still used today, although gene testing is now increasingly used to clarify the complex relationships between species and to solve many long-standing identification issues.

Within this system, vertebrates (animals with backbones) that breathe air and give birth to live young are called

A split second before reaching its destination, the sugar glider folds in its arms and legs to ensure a safe landing.

Sharp claws sink in to the tree trunk, to prevent the force of impact from throwing the aeronaut off his perch.

mammals. These young are suckled by milk from the females' mammary glands. Marsupials are an infra class (a subclass) of the mammal group, whose members typically give birth to under-developed young that continue to develop in an external pouch. Marsupials are not unique to Australasia, so this infra class is usually divided further into Australasian and American species. However, Australasia's most famous animals are undoubtedly the marsupials.

This diverse group includes species such as kangaroos, koalas, mole marsupials, Tasmanian devils, bandicoots and sugar gliders. Unlike many of their fellow marsupials, the sugar glider is not an endangered animal. Much of its

natural habitat has been lost, but the sugar glider has adapted, surviving even where little bush remains.

Sugar gliders can be found in New Guinea, on the Bismarck Archipelago, in northern and eastern Australia, in Tasmania and on nearby islands. Their ability to adapt to a wide range of habitats has made them popular pets, although this trade has now been banned in many parts of the world. In the wild, these animals are tree-dwellers and inhabit many types of woodland, although they favour eucalyptus trees, and love its sweet sap. Like many true survivors, though, they're flexible in their habits and, depending on the season, will also eat pollen, nectar, insects, larvae and small vertebrates.

Comparisons

Sugar gliders aren't the only mammals to have taken to the air. Within the sugar gliders' own genus, there are five more Australasian gliders. South-east Asia has its own gliding mammals known as colugos and there are 44 species of flying squirrel (family *Sciuridae*). All get airborne using a patagium (gliding membrane), which stretches from wrist to ankle and is opened by spreading out the limbs.

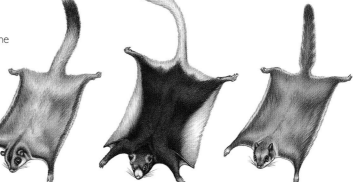

Sugar glider   Pel's scaly-tailed flying squirrel   Southern flying squirrel

ARCTIC OCEAN

Brooks Range

Mackenzie Mts

ALASKA

CANADA

LABRADOR
SEA

Rocky Mountains

NORTH
PACIFIC
OCEAN

Sierra Nevada

UNITED
STATES

Gulf of
Mexico

NORTH
ATLANTI
OCEAN

North America

North America is the world's third-largest continent, covering approximately 24,709,000 square kilometres (9,540,200 square miles) and providing a home for around 529 million people.

~

This enormous expanse of land stretches from the sandy deserts of North America to deserts of quite a different kind in the continent's icy Arctic extremes. Traditionally, Mexico and Central America are considered to be part of this great continent too, but for clarity, these will be included in the following chapter. Here, we focus on the land of the north – part of what European settlers dubbed the New World.

And is it any wonder that they chose such an evocative epithet? For people who were used to life in Europe's compact towns and family farms, this wild and wonderful continent must have looked like an giant's playground. Everywhere they went, they found nature on a monumental scale – vast peaks, colossal canyons, towering waterfalls, rivers, plains, deserts and ice-sheets that stretched as far as the eye could see. And inhabiting this strange new land were people who were every bit as fascinating as the place they called home.

Today, it's easy to imagine that cities and ranches, roads and dams have 'tamed' this once wild continent. But nature endures and, where she does, the region's biggest, baddest, wildest and strangest animals can still be found. From the Arctic Circle to the Gulf of Mexico, from bee-sized birds to flying mammals, the North American experience is one full of the strange and the unexpected.

American Bullfrog

American bullfrogs have a curious claim to fame. These wide-mouthed amphibians will attempt to make a meal out of almost anything they can cram into their mouths – from insects to other frogs! Yet their appetites aren't the only surprising thing about these bulky amphibians.

Key Facts	ORDER *Anura* / FAMILY *Ranidae* / GENUS & SPECIES *Rana catesbeiana*
Weight	Up to 500g (1.1lb)
Length	Up to 20cm (7.9in) Legs: up to 25cm (9.8in)
Sexual maturity	2–4 years
Spawning season	May–June in north; Feb–Oct in south
Number of eggs	20,000
Incubation period	Aprox 5 days
Breeding interval	Yearly
Typical diet	Insects, invertebrates, small reptiles and fish
Lifespan	Up to 10 years in the wild; 16 in captivity

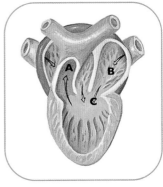

Heart

Frog and human hearts have two atria (A and B). However, frogs have just one ventricle (C) while humans have two.

Feet

Five digits on each of the bullfrogs' hind feet are joined by webbing, which helps to power them through water.

Ears

These distinctive circles behind the eyes are the frogs' eardrums. In males, the tympanum is larger than in females.

American bullfrog habitats

Everything about the American bullfrog is big. On average, these fantastic, greenish-brown amphibians grow to 7.6-15.2cm (3-6in), but there are records of them reaching 20cm (7.9in). That officially makes them North America's biggest frog. But what's really remarkable is that these big 'bulls' start out as an egg no larger than a bead!

Bullfrogs are naturally solitary creatures and gather together only during the mating season. Then, the males stake out territories and begin to defend them by calling

out their trademark 'jug-o-rum' bellow. After mating, females lay a momentous mass of tiny eggs – about 20,000 – which lie in a film on the water's surface. Males fertilize them and, within five days, tiny tadpoles begin to hatch and take to the water.

Like most amphibians, frogs undergo an amazing metamorphosis (form change) from tadpole to adult. As newly hatched tadpoles, they have external gills, no legs and an elongated body, tipped with a fleshy tail. Gills tend to be the first part of the frog to change. These are quickly covered with gill sacs, and lungs develop, which enable the frogs to breathe out of water. Then, legs start to grow and the tail is slowly reabsorbed into the body.

For bullfrogs, a complete metamorphosis can take from a few months to a few years, depending on the locality. An extended tadpole stage is good for the frog because it produces a larger adult, which offers a better chance of survival. American bullfrogs are amazingly long-lived. They live longer in warmer regions, but 10 years is average and, during that time, they'll munch their way through a surprising variety of prey!

Big bellies

American bullfrogs are one of the most widely spread species of North American amphibians. Although they don't tolerate cold very well, naturally, they can be found in freshwater ponds, lakes and marshes from southern Québec, Canada, through to Mexico and Cuba. Populations are also found in Europe, Asia and Australia

Comparisons

When the weather turns cold, American bullfrogs huddle up and hibernate. Their African counterparts, *Pyxicephalus adspersus*, have a different problem. African summers are dry and amphibians need to stay wet to breathe. So, they enter an hibernation-like state called

aestivation. By digging themselves into the mud and surrounding their bodies in a water-tight sac, they sleep the summer away, awaking when the rains return.

African bullfrog

American bullfrog

These big 'bulls' are very territorial, using their loud, distinctive calls to attract mates and proclaim ownership of territory.

A young male is unimpressed by so much 'hot air' and decides to challenge the resident to a contest of strength.

Rearing up on their powerful hind legs, the two males go for a grapple – pushing at each other like over-inflated wrestlers.

Having seen the ruckus, another bull decides discretion is the better part of valour and sneaks past the combative male!

and wherever they go, these big beasts have created big environmental problems.

All ecosystems are delicately balanced and when new species are introduced, it often results in a dramatic fall in native species. Sometimes this is because the new species brings disease, but usually the native animals simply have no defence against the intruders. In North America, populations of bullfrogs were introduced to the Pacific north-west in the early 1930s. They are bigger than the local species of frog, so they have now displaced them in many areas. It's not just a matter of size, either. North American bullfrogs are famously predatory and one study, in 1913, suggested that they will eat any animal they can overpower and fit into their ample mouths.

Indeed, a bullfrog on the attack is a startling sight. They can leap up to 2m (6.6ft) and once they're within striking distance, they lunge at their prey with their mouth open, and their fleshy tongue ready to engulf their victim. If the prey struggles too much, the frog may dive into the water with it – the struggle soon stops.

Any victim that can't be swallowed whole or pulled in with the tongue is crammed into their mouths with the fore arms. This is such an efficient technique that examinations of the contents of bullfrog stomachs have revealed rodents, turtles, snakes, birds, bats and even other bullfrogs. Unfortunately, these greedy guts do sometimes bite off more than they can chew, and many bullfrogs die by choking to death!

American Cockroach

The ancestors of the humble 'roach appeared during the Carboniferous Period, 354–295 million years ago. Since then, these hardy insects have thrived. Today, they can be found almost everywhere there's a human settlement – and their survival is thanks to some amazing adaptations.

Wing cases
A set of stiff fore wings form a 'wing case' that covers and protects the insects' delicate hind wings.

Antennae
Long antennae are believed to be sensory organs for finding food, although exactly how well they sense is unknown.

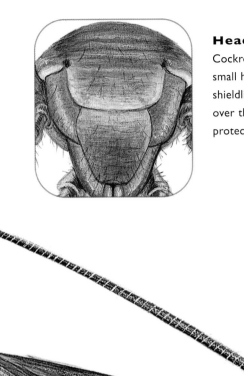

Head

Cockroaches have a relatively small head. A large, smooth, shieldlike pronotum projects over the head to give it protection.

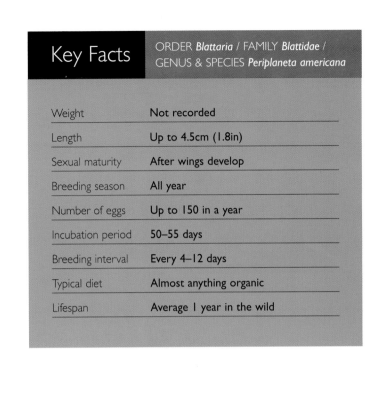

Key Facts	ORDER *Blattaria* / FAMILY *Blattidae* / GENUS & SPECIES *Periplaneta americana*
Weight	Not recorded
Length	Up to 4.5cm (1.8in)
Sexual maturity	After wings develop
Breeding season	All year
Number of eggs	Up to 150 in a year
Incubation period	50–55 days
Breeding interval	Every 4–12 days
Typical diet	Almost anything organic
Lifespan	Average 1 year in the wild

In Marvel Comics' Spiderman stories, Peter Parker is bitten by a radioactive spider and gains spider-like powers. It's unlikely that a comic book character called 'Roachman would have been as popular as Spidey, but, in the insect world, it's cockroaches that are the true superheroes.

Cockroaches belong to the scientific order *Blattaria*. Although they're regarded as pests, only around 30 species out of 4000 are found around human settlements, and only four are widespread. Of these four (the American, German, Australian and Oriental cockroaches), the American are the largest.

Like all 'roaches, American cockroaches have a flattened body, long legs and a small head, which is protected by a tough pronotum. Naturally these reddish-brown insects prefer warm, tropical habitats. They're happy, though, to inhabit any heated building, regardless of its location. In the Americas, they can be found as far north as Montreal, in Canada.

Most cockroaches are nocturnal and will actively run away from light – and they do so at super speeds. American 'roaches have been timed travelling at up to 5.4km/h (3.4mph), which is equivalent to a human running 330km/h (205mph)!

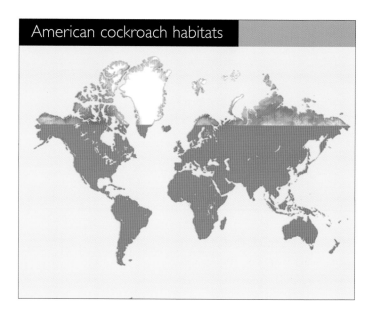

American cockroach habitats

They also have remarkable physical strength and endurance. They can climb vertical surfaces with ease, survive being submerged in water for up to 30 minutes, and live on the most meagre rations. They're able to eat almost anything organic and, if times are especially tough, they can survive without food for three weeks and without water for one week. They're even tolerant to radiation. It takes between six and fifteen times more radiation to kill a 'roach than it does to kill a human. Oh, and a cockroach that has been decapitated can survive for several weeks.

Incredible insects

'Roaches are fast, strong and resilient, but did you know that they are also intelligent?

In 2007, researchers at Tohoku University's Graduate School of Life Sciences in Japan were amazed to find that cockroaches could be trained to exhibit Pavlovian

Comparisons

Despite their name, American, German (*Blatta germanica*) and Australian cockroaches (*Periplaneta australasiae*) all originated in Africa. Only the flightless Oriental cockroach (*Blatta orientalis*) lives up to its name and comes from Asia. There are an estimated 4000 species of cockroach, but these four are skilled stowaways. Wherever people have gone, they've travelled with them, and this now accounts for most of the world's cockroach infestations.

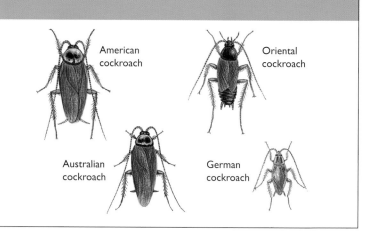

American cockroach

Oriental cockroach

Australian cockroach

German cockroach

responses to stimuli. Ivan Petrovich Pavlov (1849–1936) was a Russian psychologist, famous for his work on conditioned reflexes. In a series of experiments in 1901, Pavlov gave food to dogs every time a bell rang or a whistle was blown (other stimuli were also used). The dogs began to associate the stimuli with the arrival of food and would salivate even if they heard the noise and no food was given.

The Japanese researchers were stunned to find that cockroaches responded in the same way. In their tests, they exposed cockroaches to an odour whenever they fed them with a sugary solution. After several attempts, when the cockroaches smelt the scent, they reacted as though food was on its way. The implication is that 'roaches have a

memory and a capacity to learn – something that had previously been associated only with mammals.

Further research has shown that cockroaches seem to be able to make complex decisions, such as allocating resources to fulfil the needs of a group. In one study, 50 cockroaches were placed in a dish with three shelters, each of which could support 40 insects. Every time, the insects arranged themselves in two shelters with 25 insects in each, leaving the third shelter empty. In fact, Nicholas Strausfeld, a neurobiologist at the University of Arizona, USA, has spent much of his career examining the brain structures of tiny creatures like cockroaches, and his findings have lead him to suggest that insects may possess 'the most sophisticated brains on this planet.'

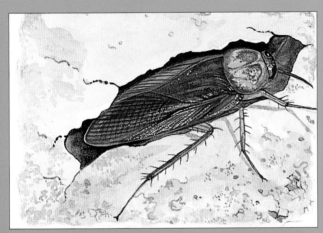

With a body designed to take cover under logs and stones, it has no trouble keeping itself concealed in a modern home.

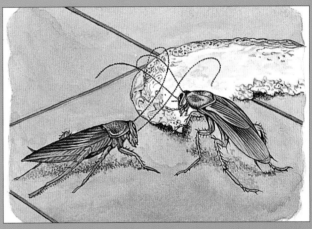

Once night falls, the 'roaches creep out of their hidey holes and start to search for food – and any food will do!

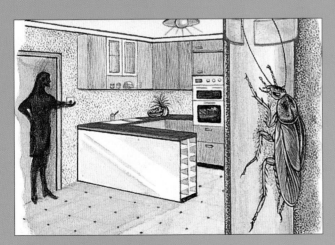

These unwanted guests are fast on their feet, but even if you catch one, there's always plenty more to take their place.

Hidden away and protected from harm inside this tough little egg case are dozens of baby 'roaches waiting to hatch.

American Mink

When they're not being farmed for their fur, they're being cursed as invasive predators. But these marvellous mammals have hidden qualities. They're amazingly adaptable and surprisingly clever. They may even give some members of the primate family a run for their money in the intelligence stakes.

Hind feet

Mink are a semi-aquatic species, making their homes around freshwater rivers and lakes. They have short legs and partial webbing on their hind feet, which makes them excellent swimmers.

Teeth

A set of long, dagger-like canine teeth are used for grasping and killing prey. Smaller, sharp carnassials behind the canines work like scissors to sheer flesh from the bone.

Key Facts	ORDER *Carnivora* / FAMILY *Mustelidae* / GENUS & SPECIES *Neovison vison*
Weight	Males: 570–1,090g (1.2–2.4lb) Females: 680–1,350g (1.5–3lb)
Length	Up to 43cm (16.9in) Tail: Up to 23cm (9in)
Sexual maturity	Average: 10 months
Breeding season	January–April
Number of young	2–6
Gestation period	27–33 days
Breeding interval	Yearly
Typical diet	Fish and small mammals
Lifespan	Up to 3 years in the wild; 12 in captivity

Predatory pest or born survivor? In recent years, the loveable mink has earned itself an unenviable reputation. These attractive animals have long been trapped for their fur, but intensive breeding on fur farms has proved to be just as contentious. While some conservationists argue that mink farming helps to protect wild populations from over-hunting, some farms have created other, unforeseen, problems. In many parts of world, there are now populations of feral American mink, descended from those animals that managed to escape captivity.

The American mink *(Neovison vison)* occupies the same environmental niche as its European counterparts *(Mustela lutreola)*, but it is generally bigger and more aggressive. Mink are solitary animals that fight to defend their territory – and will kill if necessary. The result has been

that, in many places, native European mink have been wiped out. Attempts are under way to introduce some populations of European mink onto isolated islands, where they can breed without competing directly with their American cousins, but *Neovison vison* is such a good swimmer that this has proved difficult!

In their native range, throughout Canada and the United States, these carnivores have been just as adaptable. They dislike dry, desert regions but otherwise they'll tolerate anything from Alaska's chilly tundra to Florida's steamy swamplands. They're solitary and semi-aquatic by nature. For mink, the ideal home is beside a slow-running stream, hidden by thick vegetation. They may dig their own temporary burrows or take refuge in cavities in tree roots, but often they'll make use of dens vacated by other

Mink are born opportunists, happy to eat any animal – on land or in the water – that they can overpower.

Clambering up to a handy perch gives our mink a better view of the surrounding area. And just in time too!

Plunging straight from the branch into the cool waters below, the mink catches a passing fish completely by surprise.

With its prize clamped firmly in its jaws, the mink returns to dry land to enjoy his fish supper in peace.

Comparisons

Long-tailed weasels (*Mustela frenata*) may be only 26.6cm (10.5in) long, but they're every bit as predatory as American mink. They're quick, agile and alert animals and, like their relatives, are good climbers and swimmers. Prey includes a range of small mammals, which they kill with a bite to the base of the skull – a common method of dispatch amongst the *Mustelidae* family.

Long-tailed weasel   American mink

waterside residents, like muskrat (*Ondatra zibethicus*). They're just as likely to be found in caves around rocky coastlines, too, where they take advantage of food left by successive tides. They've even found their way into the suburbs, where any intelligent animal can always survive.

Clever carnivores

American mink are members of the *Mustelidae* family. This large and diverse scientific group dates back 40 million years, and it includes many animals that, traditionally, were considered difficult to classify. Thanks to advances in gene testing, this group is now being tidied up, but at present it still includes mink, weasels, otters and ferrets.

Typically, mustelids have stocky bodies with short legs, short round ears and thick fur. Apart from sea otters, all members of this family produce a strong odour that allows solitary souls, like the mink, to communicate with others by leaving scent messages. These appealing animals also have one other characteristic in common: they're considered to be highly intelligent. This is partly because of their playful personalities. It's impossible to say exactly why some animals play and others don't, but play has long been associated with intelligence because it seems to have little to do with survival or instinct. Humans play simply because they enjoy it and it's easy to imagine that an intelligent animal gets the same rewards from play as we do.

In the wild, mustelids are also naturally inquisitive. Some species, like otters, have demonstrated problem-solving and tool-using behaviour, which is usually associated with primates. This curiosity has also enabled them to perform well in tests. In fact, in one study, mink were tested to compare their intelligence with that of ferrets, skunks and cats. Experiments were designed to test the ability of each animal to remember specific shapes – and the mink consistently came top of the class. Strangely, mink even performed better than some primate groups in certain tests. They were found to be especially good at 'task learning' and were able to repeat an activity after only one attempt.

American mink habitats

Big Brown Bat

These hardy and wide-spread bats may be common, but they are far from commonplace. Bats are the only mammals to truly master the art of flying, but it's their method of finding their way around in the dark that makes these furry fliers really remarkable.

Key Facts	ORDER *Chiroptera* / FAMILY *Vespertilionidae* / GENUS & SPECIES *Eptesicus fuscus*	
Weight	14–21g (0.5–0.7oz)	
Length	10–13cm (3.9–5.1in) Wingspan: 4–5cm (1.6–2in)	
Sexual maturity	1–2 years	
Breeding season	Autumn	
Number of young	1–2	
Gestation period	60 days	
Breeding interval	Yearly	
Typical diet	Beetles and other insects	
Lifespan	Up to 20 years in the wild	

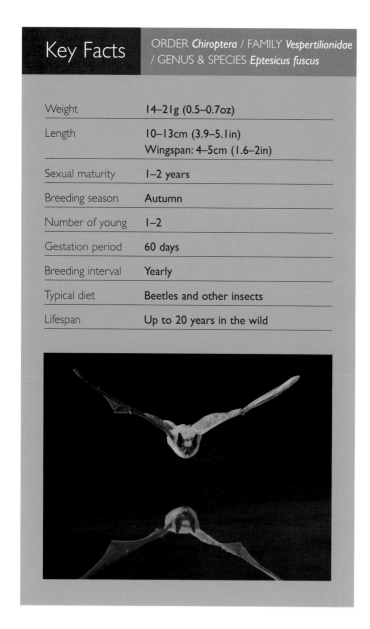

Feet

Bats' fore arms and elongated fingers form the framework for their wings. Their feet remain free to grip prey and roosts.

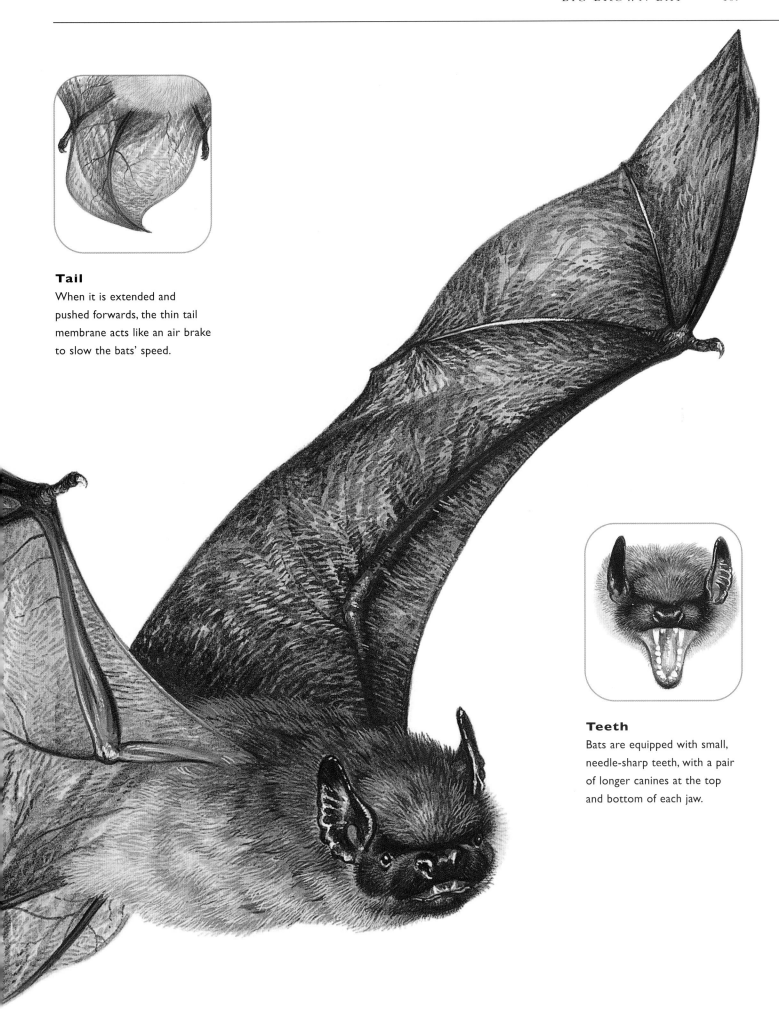

Tail

When it is extended and pushed forwards, the thin tail membrane acts like an air brake to slow the bats' speed.

Teeth

Bats are equipped with small, needle-sharp teeth, with a pair of longer canines at the top and bottom of each jaw.

Adult brown bats may be big, but their young are small and extremely vulnerable to attack from predators like owls.

This means that bat mothers have to be especially vigilant when re-entering the maternity roost after a feeding trip.

Big brown bat habitats

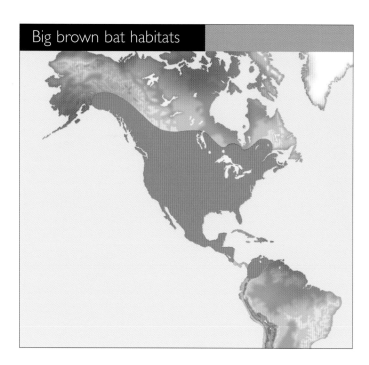

Worldwide, there are 1100 species of bat. These strange mammals may look like rodents, but gene sequencing places them in the scientific 'super group' *Laurasiatheria*. This group includes animals such as pangolins, hoofed mammals and whales, which are all believed to have evolved in Laurasia – the northern 'slice' of the great super continent, Pangaea. The oldest identified bat fossils date from the early Eocene Period, 59–34 million years ago, which is the same time that the ancestors of most modern mammals appeared.

Big brown bats are one of North America's most widespead bat species. Populations of these furry fliers are believed to occupy 48 American states, as well as parts of northern Canada, Mexico, Central America and some Caribbean islands. While many species of bat are struggling to survive, these big bats have proved to be extremely adaptable. They prefer wet woodlands but can withstand a variety of conditions, as long as there's an abundance of insect life. Trees are favourite roosts, and bats are especially welcome guests on farms, as a single colony can eat up to 33 million root worms each summer!

Once winter arrives and food becomes scarce, many mammals hibernate. By lowering their metabolism – reducing their body temperature and slowing their breathing – they are able to enter a sleeplike state, which conserves energy. In warmer areas, large brown bats have no need to hibernate, but those that live in cooler climates spend December to April holed up in their roosts until spring. Even though they mate in the autumn, female bats postpone gestation during these harsh winter months. Using a physical adaptation called delayed implantation, they ensure that their young are born only once warm weather, and a good food supply, is assured.

Strange sounds
One of the keys to the success of the big brown bats is their ability to navigate and hunt in the dark.

Despite the well-known saying 'as blind as a bat', these flying mammals aren't really blind. Many see quite well and have excellent hearing, but some species rely on

Squeezing into the secluded farm building through a hole in the roof, she first double-checks for danger.

Soon she is back with the rest of the colony, eagerly licking the faces of her young to bond with them.

Comparisons

There's something undeniably cute about the big brown bats' almost doglike face, but you'd have to be a bit batty to find South America's wrinkled-face bat (*Centurio senex*) as appealing. In fact, these odd mammals cover their own faces up when they're resting. They do this by pulling the excess skin from their chin over their head, although no one knows they do it!

Big brown bat

Wrinkled-face bat

another 'sense' entirely for getting around. This 'sixth sense' is called echolocation. Microbats (those belonging to the suborder *Microchiroptera*) aren't the only animals to use this strange ability. At least two groups of birds echolocate, as do, more famously, whales. However, microbats have become masters of the art. Their echolocation is so accurate they can skim moths off the surface of the water and avoid silk-thin spiders' webs, spun between the tops of the trees.

Echolocating works by using echoes to build up a 3D picture of the world in sound. In the case of microbats, the process begins with a series of ultrasound clicks, which they generate through their open mouths. When these clicks hit an object – up to 17m (55.8ft) in front of them – the bats can judge their location and distance from the object based on how long it takes to hear the returning echo. Many species of microbats make their own distinct and identifiable clicks, but these are typically beyond the range of human hearing and can be picked up only using a bat detector. With a good detector, it's even possible to tune in to specific species.

Some microbats use their noses as well as their mouths to produce clicks, but big brown bats have small noses. So, to improve their ultrasound 'beam', they shout! Big brown bats and hoary bats (*Lasiurus cinereus*) are the only bats that produce audible noises in flight.

Great Grey Shrike

Shrike may be appealing-looking birds, but they are famous for their less than appealing eating habits. While most species of hunting birds devour their prey as soon as they have caught it, great grey shrike are peculiar predators and store their kills on a gruesome gibbet.

Key Facts	ORDER *Passeriformes* / FAMILY *Laniidae* / GENUS & SPECIES *Lanius excubitor*	
Weight	Up to 68g (2.4oz)	
Length	22–26cm (8.6–10.2in) Wingspan: 32cm (12.6in)	
Sexual maturity	1 year	
Breeding season	March–May, but varies across range	
Number of eggs	4–7	
Incubation period	15–17 days	
Breeding interval	1–2 broods a year	
Typical diet	Small mammals, birds and insects	
Lifespan	Up to 10 years in the wild	

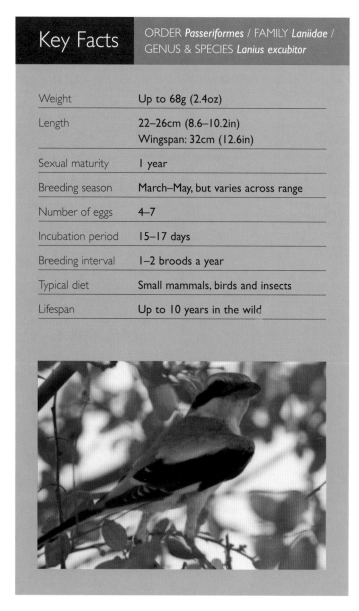

Juvenile
Young shrike are greyish brown above, with distinct barring on their under parts. This makes it easier for them to blend with their surroundings.

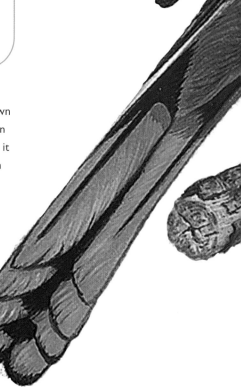

Bill

It's believed that some great grey shrike dispatch their victims with a blow to the head, using their hooked bill.

Feet

Three long, forwards-facing toes and one shorter, backwards-facing toe is the typical, anisodactyl, layout for the feet of perching birds.

With their pearl-grey upper parts, snowy under parts and bold eye stripe, great grey shrikes are strikingly handsome birds. Similar in size to the North American wood thrush (*Hylocichla mustelina*), shrikes are stockier, with a long, broad tail and a pronounced hooked bill. Yet, despite their winning looks and tuneful, warbling calls, they have some very nasty habits In Latin, their scientific name *Lanius excubitor* means 'sentinel butcher', but most bird-watchers simply call them 'butcher birds'!

These predatory passerines (perching birds) are flexible in their choice of habitats. They breed in Europe, Asia, Africa and North America as far as the Arctic Circle. They prefer semi-woodland environments, heaths and farmlands – anywhere with trees, scattered bushes or high vantage points, like telegraph poles. It's here that they are most often seen, standing bolt upright, scanning the ground for prey. They are also able to 'hover' in the air like kestrels, and may do this for up to 20 minutes at a time.

Once prey has been spotted, shrike are quick to demonstrate their aerial prowess. Ordinarily they have an undulating, up-and-down flight pattern but, when chasing prey, they swoop like a hawk. This is such a fast and decisive form of attack that they are able to grab insects from the air, and even small birds may be taken this way – the shrikes attack from below and seize the bird's feet in their bill. When tackling earthbound prey, they quickly drop to the ground and pin their victims down. Usually they attack small rodents, but they have been known to attack creatures as large as the ermine. It's believed that some shrike dispatch their prey with a blow to the head from their hooked bill. However, it's what

Great grey shrike habitats

Comparisons

West Africa's fiery-breasted bush-shrike (*Malaconotus cruentus*) may be similar in shape and size to the great grey shrike, but the two species couldn't look more different. As their name suggests, great grey shrike have an almost monochrome grey and white plumage. In contrast, the fiery-breasted bush-shrike well deserve their evocative name, with lively, olive-yellow upper parts and a dazzling, bold flash of orange-red on the breast.

Great grey shrike

Fiery-breasted bush-shrike

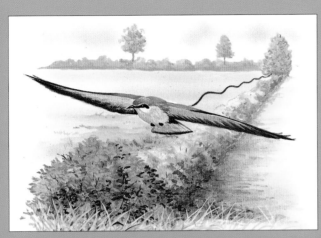

Swooping low, the shrike scans the ground for a midday meal. Its keen eyes spot something interesting in the distance.

A small flock of sparrows are busy enjoying a dust bath – oblivious to the danger that threatens them.

Before they can react, the shrike hits home, pinning one of the sparrows down as the rest of the flock scatter.

The hunting has been good recently, but rather than waste a tasty treat he impales it on a thorn to consume later.

happens next that has earned these handsome birds such a gruesome nickname.

Butcher birds

Unlike large predatory birds, shrike don't have talons. This makes it difficult to carry prey, so they juggle it! The Irish ornithologist Francis Orpen Morris (1810-93) described this in his 1891 book on British birds. Shrikes enjoy a varied diet and are particularly fond of insects, such as beetles, but, as Morris observed, they will also tackle 'shrew and other mice, small birds, and occasionally even partridges, fieldfares, and … reptiles, such as lizards and frogs … but when carrying a mouse or a bird some distance, shrike shift it alternately from the bill to the mouth, as an alleviation of the weight.'

Once at their feeding site, it becomes clear why shrikes are called butcher birds. They impale the bodies of their dead victims on thorn bushes, like butchers hanging up meat on a hook. In Europe, the spines of blackthorn (sloe) bush are used, but barbed wire will do just as well. This may seem gory but, for the shrike, it's a practical solution to an everyday problem. As Morris observed, their feet aren't strong enough to hold their prey. So, a spike secures the corpse while they pull it apart with their bill. Interestingly, it's not instinctive behaviour, which means they must learn the technique by trial and error. Once they've mastered it, though, a much wider range of food is at hand for their consumption, and they can store excess food as well. Males even impale inedible items, to make themselves look like successful hunters to available females.

Mantis

Are these innocent-looking insects really cannibals? For decades, it was believed that females devoured males during mating. The real truth about these marvellous mantids has now been revealed and, while it might not be as gruesome as we once thought, it is just as amazing.

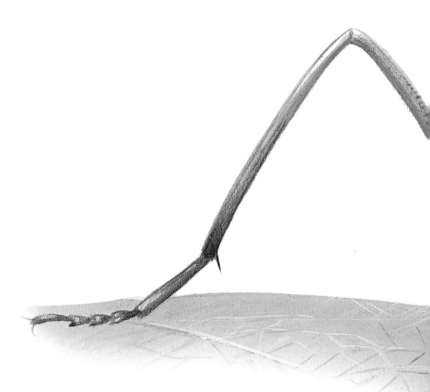

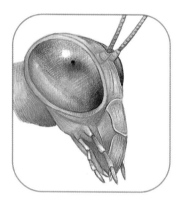

Head
Mantids are one of the few insects who can manoeuvre their heads to look over their shoulders for danger.

Fore legs
Mantises have a pair of grasping fore limbs, which are called raptorial legs. These are used to hold prey securely.

Wings
Four wings open with a fanlike motion when the mantises take to the air. At rest, they lie along the body.

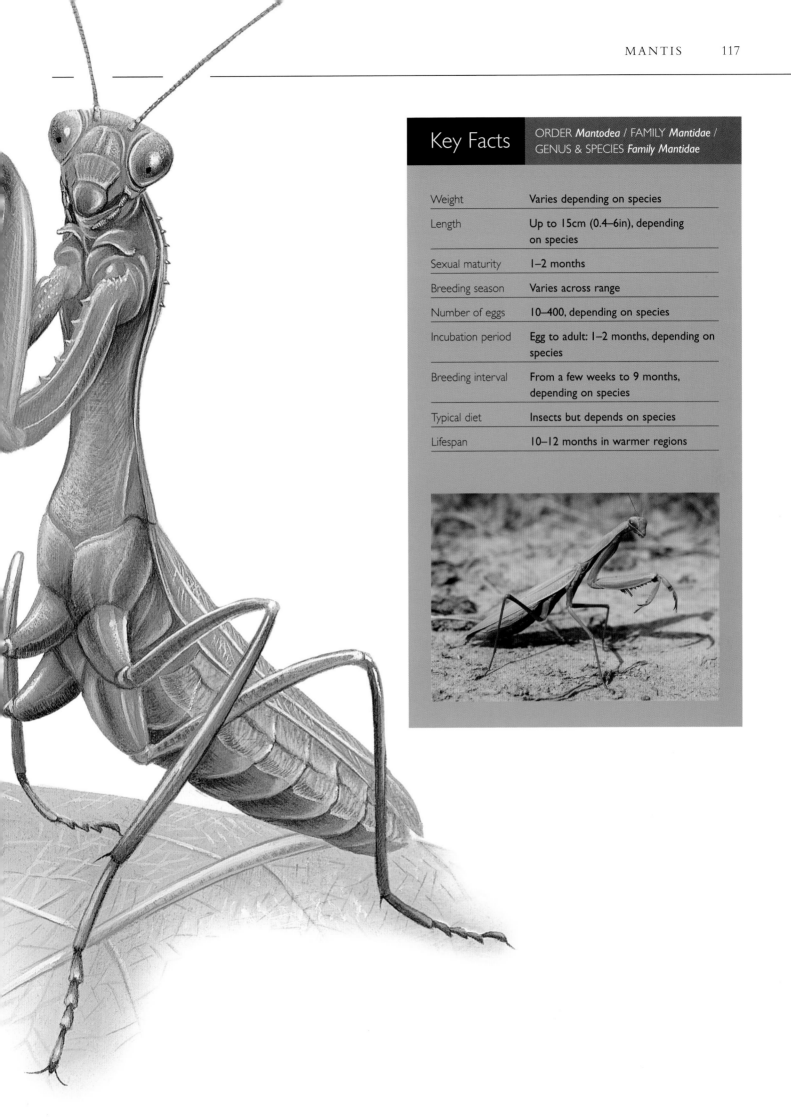

Key Facts

ORDER *Mantodea* / **FAMILY** *Mantidae* / **GENUS & SPECIES** *Family Mantidae*

Weight	Varies depending on species
Length	Up to 15cm (0.4–6in), depending on species
Sexual maturity	1–2 months
Breeding season	Varies across range
Number of eggs	10–400, depending on species
Incubation period	Egg to adult: 1–2 months, depending on species
Breeding interval	From a few weeks to 9 months, depending on species
Typical diet	Insects but depends on species
Lifespan	10–12 months in warmer regions

Mantis habitats

The female mantis, or mantid, has a reputation as 'man-eaters'. It used to be believed that she devoured the male during mating by biting off his head, as she does with prey. Numerous studies suggested that not only was such sexual cannibalism normal for mantids but that it was necessary because it was only during the male's death throes that his sperm (reproductive cells) would be passed on.

Cannibalism isn't unknown in nature – in fact, it's alarmingly common. An estimated 1500 animal species are thought to indulge in some form of cannibalism. This list includes some of nature's simplest organisms, the nematodes, as well as our closest relatives, chimpanzees. Some animals resort to cannibalism to survive, but the reasons for such aberrant behaviour are many and complex. Males often do it to dispose of a rival's offspring. Females sometimes do it to reduce the number of young in their care when food is scarce. Mouse mothers have been known to eat their whole litter when they're stressed. Sexual cannibalism is especially common in the insect world. Redback spiders, black widows and scorpions are known to kill their mates during or after sex, but it now seems that the bad reputation of female mantids is mostly undeserved.

In nature, a male who wants to mate will generally approach a female and – if she is interested – some type of courtship ritual will take place. What was discovered, in study by Liske and Davis in 1987, was that the mantids' cannibalistic behaviour wasn't natural, but a response to being caged and observed! It was a ground-breaking study and many enthusiastic entomologists (scientists who study insects) have since followed their work.

Getting in the mood

Liske and Davis began their study by subtly altering the captive mantids' environment. They fed the insects more regularly, kept the lights low, and then allowed them to mate in a darkened room, watched by cameras rather than

Comparisons

Vivid pinks, greens and fancy body decorations help the flower mantids (family *Hymenopodidae*) to perfectly blend in with the flowers on which they perch. However, don't be misled. These colourful creatures aren't vegetarians. Like their praying mantis relatives, they're carnivores and are equipped with strong fore legs for capturing prey, and small but powerful jaws to tear their victims' bodies apart.

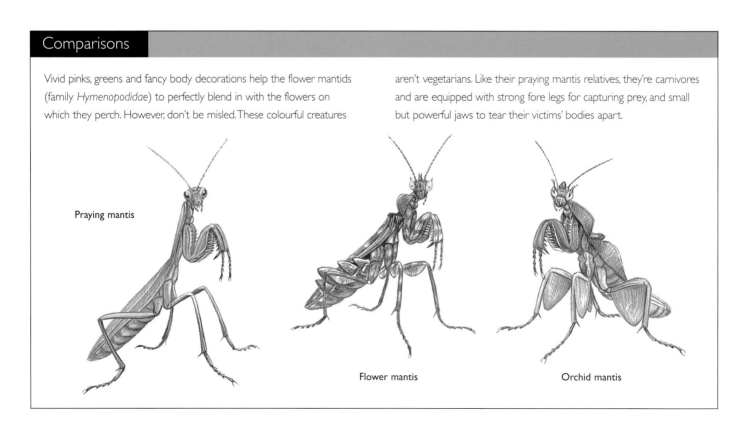

Praying mantis

Flower mantis

Orchid mantis

surrounded by people constantly moving and distracting them. Out of 30 matings, there were no deaths. More surprisingly, the cameras were able to record an elaborate mating ritual, involving both the male and female, which was previously unknown to science.

Mantids are ambush hunters. Perfectly camouflaged, fast and powerful, they react quickly and decisively to sudden movements, especially when they're hungry. Typically it will take less than one-tenth of a second for a mantid to spot and seize prey. So it would seem sensible for them to evolve some form of courtship ritual that enables males to approach hungry females without ending up on the menu!

The work of Liske and Davis suggests that these rituals get disrupted when hungry and stressed insects are subjected to laboratory conditions. They have a large range of vision, so will notice activity in the laboratory. In the wild, males also have the chance to try their luck elsewhere if a female isn't interested. In a cage, they have no choice but to stay where they are. The urge to mate is a powerful one but a desperate male, forcing his attentions of an unresponsive female, risks incurring her wrath.

There are more than 2000 species of mantids, and since this study, there has been much debate about the role of sexual cannibalism within the family. It's clear that, in some species, females do devour males during mating, but this is far from common. What's more, mantid behaviour has been shown to be much more complex than was previously thought.

With such superb cryptic camouflage, this mantis can easily creep closer to its unwary neighbour without being spotted.

With a sudden spring, the mantis snaps its fore legs shut, trapping its victim's struggling body within its spiky embrace.

Held in his captors' vicelike grip, there's no escape for this little mantid as he's drawn upwards, towards the waiting jaws.

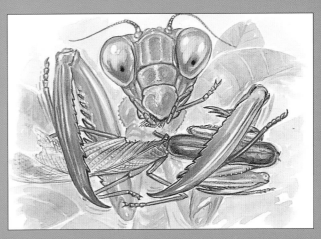

The predator quickly splits open its victim's hard outer shell — making it easier to get at the soft flesh inside.

Southern Flying Squirrel

Despite their name, these strange North American squirrels don't really fly.
Instead they glide gracefully from tree trunk to tree trunk, using a special
membrane called a patagium to catch the air as they fall – just like a parachutist
using a canopy to break their descent.

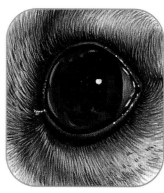

Eyes

A pair of huge, forwards-facing
eyes ensures that these small
squirrels have excellent
binocular vision. This enables
them to judge distances more
accurately when leaping from
tree to tree.

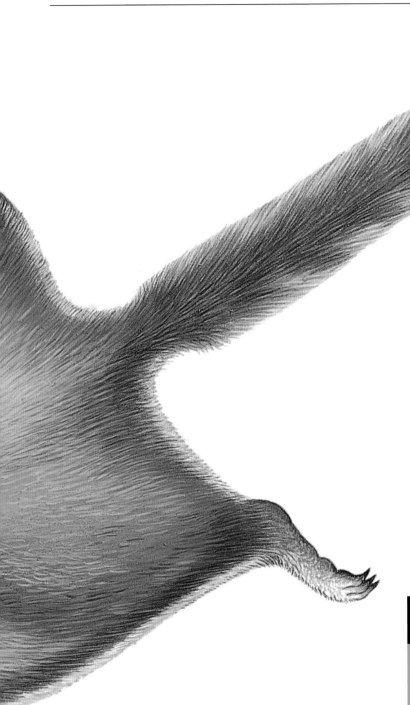

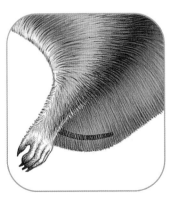

Wrist extensions
Tiny rods of thin cartilage
(a form of stiff connective
tissue) project from the
squirrels' wrists. These help
to support the leading edge of
the all-important patagium
(gliding membrane).

Key Facts	ORDER *Rodentia* / FAMILY *Sciuridae* / GENUS & SPECIES *Glaucomys volans*
Weight	Up to 225g (7.9oz)
Length	Up to 28cm (11in) excluding tail
Sexual maturity	Females: 9 months
Breeding season	Winter, but varies with location
Number of young	2–6
Gestation period	40 days
Breeding interval	Twice a year possible
Typical diet	Nuts, seeds, fruit, insects and birds' eggs
Lifespan	Up to 6 years in the wild; 13 in captivity

According to a fossil found in China in 2006, mammals may have actually taken to the skies at around the same time as birds were developing the ability to fly. What's more, it is believed that the squirrel-sized ancestor of today's gliders – known as *Volaticotherium antiquum* – got around in just the same way, using a membrane to flit from perch to perch.

Flying is controlled movement through the air. By contrast, gliding animals are dependent on gravity. Once they have become airborne, achieving control over their 'flight' is difficult, although they can direct their glide by tensing their bodies and flapping their tails. This may make gliding seem like a poor substitute for true flight, but it's a remarkably efficient way of getting around. Depending on the air currents, southern flying squirrels can glide as far as 45m (147.6ft). Landing is no problem, either. As squirrels approach their destination, they flip up their tail and raise their body back to slow their speed, giving themselves time to position their feet for a safe touchdown.

These cute creatures are most at home in woodlands and can be found in south-eastern parts of Canada and eastern parts of North America. Populations are also found in the tropical forests of Mexico and Honduras. Here, amongst the benefits and threats inherent in all woodlands, their gliding lifestyle comes into its own. Stuck on the forest floor, these little mammals would be vulnerable to attack. Even in the tree tops, there's no guarantee of safety. So, being able to take to the air when predators appear, or to glide from one food source to another without danger, is a

It's always a good idea to look before you leap, and that's exactly what this flying squirrel is doing!

Once he's sure of his distance and direction, it's time for take off, but gliding does have some disadvantages over flying …

Now that the little squirrel is airborne, he can't change direction quickly, even though danger is heading his way.

Time for a quick landing! Dropping down to the nearest tree, our squirrel scurries towards a convenient bolt hole.

Comparisons

Southern flying squirrels are competent gliders, but south-east Asia's colugos (family *Cynocephalidae*) are real exponents of the art. The squirrels' patagium is a square sheet of muscle attached to the wrists and ankles, but the colugos' gliding membrane is much more substantial. Additional skin stretches between the both hind legs and the tail, creating a kite shape that makes it more efficient in the air.

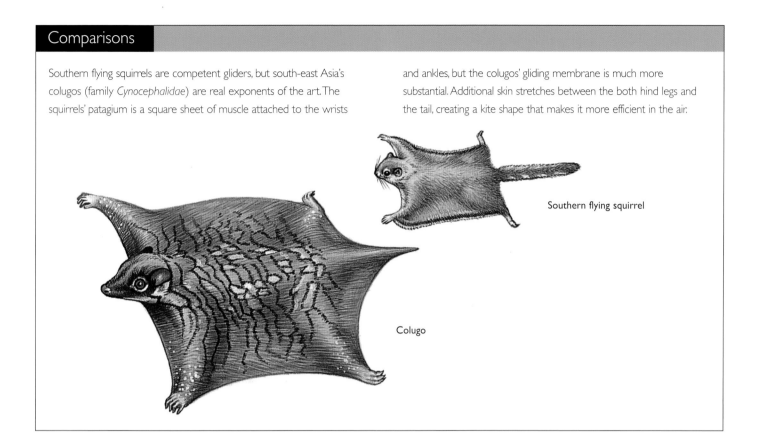

Southern flying squirrel

Colugo

Southern flying squirrel habitats

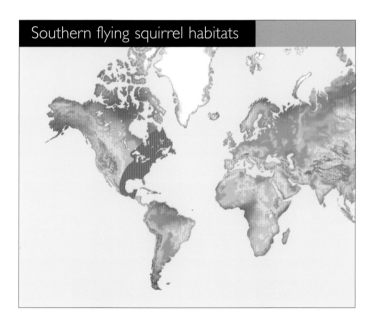

great advantage. A further benefit is that gliding uses much less energy than flying.

Sociable squirrels

Most animals are highly territorial and will only share space with other members of their own, extended families. Some species are so anti-social that they don't even like each other! American mink (*Neovison vison*) for instance are naturally solitary and can only tolerate each other during the breeding season. In comparison, southern flying squirrels seem like party animals! In the south of their range, they will usually feed and nest alone, but in the cooler north, where sharing body warmth with others helps to conserve energy, they can often be found in groups of up to 20 or more. There are even reports of flying squirrels hunkering down with other species like screech-owls (genus *Megascops*) and bats.

In the wild, these large-eyed mammals usually live in woodlands, where they nest in tree hollows, often those discarded by woodpeckers. However, they are a very adaptable species and any available hideaway makes an acceptable home. They're quite comfortable in bird boxes, out-buildings and attics. By day, they spend much of their time asleep, either in a tree cavity or a purpose-built nest. When night falls, they emerge from cover to feed. Using their gliding membrane to travel from tree to tree, these amazing animals can cover great distances on foraging expeditions and enjoy a varied diet as a result. Seeds, fruit and the nuts from trees such as hickory, red and white oak, and beech are all favourites, but these perky mammals will take bird's eggs, insects and carrion if it's easy to access. Like all squirrels, they store any excess food, especially acorns, for the winter when they lie low and eke out the supplies they accumulated during the good weather.

CENTRAL
AMERICA

CARIBBEAN SEA

Amazon
Basin

SOUTH
AMERICA

Andes

SOUTH PACIFIC
OCEAN

Patagonia

SOUTH
ATLANTI
OCEAN

Central and South America

Mexico, Central and South America, and the beautiful islands of the
Caribbean are often collectively referred to as Latin America.

This is a term used to define those nations where languages based on Latin – primarily French, Spanish and Portuguese – are predominant. Yet, historically and culturally, this remarkable region is perhaps one of the world's most diverse and dynamic.

Covering approximately 21,069,501 square kilometres (8,135,000 square miles), Latin America begins in Mexico, then snakes down through Guatemala and Belize to Nicaragua, Costa Rica, El Salvador and Panama, which form the bulk of the Central American landmass. Columbia is where South America 'proper' begins. This massive ear of land sits between the Atlantic and Pacific Oceans, providing a home to 13 nations and more than 371 million people. It's a land of wild beauty and natural wonders. It's here that we find the Andes, the world's longest mountain chain, and the Amazon, the world's biggest rainforest. Within these environments, a quarter of all the world's animals live, including some genuine animal record-breakers – the anaconda, the world's heaviest snake; the goliath tarantula, the biggest spider; and the Galapagos tortoise, the largest tortoise.

In this section we'll be investigating some of the region's amazing animal inhabitants in greater detail. Some of them, like the red howler monkey, may not be the biggest or the heaviest, but are just as memorable! Some have bodies that have adapted to life in river, jungle or mountain in weird and wonderful ways. And some, as we'll discover, have much more curious claims to fame.

Emperor Tamarin

With their stupendous, snowy moustaches, emperor tamarins are one of the most curious of South America's primate species. They lack a number of the physical advantages that many apes and monkeys take for granted, but other adaptations mean these tiny tamarins do surprisingly well for themselves.

Key Facts	ORDER *Primates* / FAMILY *Callitrichidae* / GENUS & SPECIES *Saguinus imperator*	
Weight	Up to 400g (14.1oz)	
Length	Up to 26cm (10.2in) Tail: up to 41cm (16.1in)	
Sexual maturity	16–20 months	
Spawning season	All year	
Number of young	2	
Gestation period	140–145 days	
Breeding interval	Yearly	
Typical diet	Dry season: fruit Wet season: nectar and small insects	
Lifespan	Up to 12 years in the wild; 17 in captivity	

Fore paws
Five long fingers are used to grip on to branches. A set of long claws help to anchor the tamarin in place.

Teeth
Tamarins eat insects and small vertebrates, but these impressive canines are used mainly to pierce tough fruit rather then tear flesh.

Feet
The emperor tamarins' short toilet claw is used during mutual grooming , which is an important part of troop bonding sessions.

Emperor tamarin habitats

What's the difference between a monkey and an ape?

Monkeys and apes are both members of the scientific order Primates. Apes, galagos, lemurs, lorisids, monkeys, tarsiers and great apes, including humans, are all primates. Although physical characteristics vary greatly between the species, most primates share several well-known traits. First is their intelligence. Primates tend to have a domed skull, which protects a large and complex brain. Secondly, they have five digits on their hands and feet (a pentadactyly design). These hands are highly mobile and dextrous.

Usually, primates have flat nails rather than claws, which allows for the development of sensitive fingertips. They also tend to have opposable thumbs, which can be moved to 'oppose' each finger in turn, helping them to manipulate objects.

Monkeys and apes share many of these features. The most obvious difference between the two is that monkeys, like tamarins, have tails and apes don't. Apes also tend to have bodies that can be held upright, with long arms and flexible shoulder blades that let them brachiate (swing from branch to branch). Monkeys usually move about on all fours, using their tails for added grip and balance.

Tamarins, though, are peculiar primates. They don't have opposable thumbs or nails. Their long feet are adapted for running along branches, and so for added grip they have claws on their fingers and toes – apart from the toilet claw, which is used for personal grooming. Because they're monkeys, and not apes, they do have tails, but these aren't prehensile (gripping). Instead, they're used like rudders, to steady the tamarins as they run from branch to branch. Once again, this is quite strange because most New World monkeys have prehensile tails. (Old World species from Africa and Asia generally don't.)

Flexible feeders

Emperor tamarins may not have sensitive hands or prehensile tails, but these moustachioed monkeys have adapted well to life in the Amazon Basin.

Tamarin troops live in extended family groups, dominated by one breeding female, her mate, other males

Comparisons

A wild array of manes and moustaches make tamarins look like extravagantly dressed dandies. The emperor tamarin was named after a nineteenth-century German emperor who sported similarly stupendous face decoration. However, the emperors' moustaches look modest when compared to the sideburns and striped headwear of Geoffroy's tamarin (*Saguinus geoffroyi*), or the wild, rock-star haircut of the cotton-top tamarin (*Saguinus oedipus*).

Emperor tamarin

Geoffroy's tamarin

Cotton-top tamarin

Perching high in the tree canopy, the emperor tamarin troop enjoys a unrivalled, panoramic view of the surrounding area.

Emperors are territorial but tolerate the presence of another group of tamarins – saddlebacks (*Saguinus fuscicollis*).

Saddlebacks have a different diet to the emperors, so they present no real threat. They also help to keep a lookout for danger.

While emperors scan the air, saddlebacks watch the ground. If predators are spotted, both troops call out warnings – and everybody runs!

and their young. Working together, this group stakes out a piece of prime real estate and diligently defends it from intruders. Traditionally tamarin territories are large, covering about 30–40 hectares (74.1–98.8 acres) and, over the course of a day, the troop will wander across one-third of it. Within each territory is everything that they need to survive and thrive.

Although logging has disrupted their traditional homelands and reduced their numbers dramatically, tamarin populations can still be found in the south-west of the Amazon Basin, eastern Peru, northern Bolivia, and two states of western Brazil. Here they occupy several levels of the forest, from the towering tree tops to the lower crowns of young trees. Fruit is their main food but,

as the year progresses, they adapt their diet to take advantage of whatever is plentiful. Leaves, flowers, nectar, insects and insect larvae are all actively eaten as well as the occasional small lizard, frog or bird's egg that may come their way.

Emperors are diurnal, so most food-gathering takes place during the day. Like most primates, they have excellent binocular vision, which helps them to judge distances accurately and so hunt more efficiently. Tamarins are also very small, which may seem like a disadvantage in a land where big bad predators abound, but being light has its plus points too. It allows them to creep to the very tips of tree branches, where the newly grown, succulent leaves and buds can be found.

Giant Otter

Giant otters are one of South America's astounding animal record-breakers. These charming 'water dogs' are the longest, most powerful otter species, but being big isn't their only claim to fame. These proficient predators have learnt that, by working together, they can tackle almost any other jungle giant.

Skull

A streamlined skull is lined with rows of razor-sharp teeth. These help the otters to grip wet, wriggling food like fish.

Tail
The otters' scientific name, *Pteronura brasiliensis*, means Brazilian wing-tail, referring to their flattened tail, which helps generate thrust when they swim.

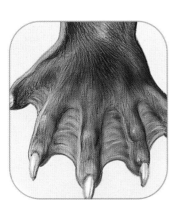

Webs and claws
Four short, stocky legs end in a set of large, well-webbed paws. These, in turn, are tipped with sharp claws.

Key Facts	ORDER *Carnivora* / FAMILY *Mustelidae* / GENUS & SPECIES *Pteronura brasiliensis*
Weight	Up to 34kg (75lb)
Length	Up to 2m (6.6ft) including tail
Sexual maturity	2 years
Breeding season	All year
Number of young	1–6; usually 2
Gestation period	52–79 days
Breeding interval	7–33 months, depending on conditions
Typical diet	Fish and crustaceans
Lifespan	Up to 8 years in the wild; 17 in captivity

An animal can grow as big as its ecosystem can support – and the Amazon Rainforest can support some real giants. This immense region stretches across nine nations and contains around 5.5 million square kilometres (1.4 billion acres) of wet, broadleaf forest. Running through this natural wonder is the magnificent Amazon River, which flows for over 6437km (4000 miles). In the dry season, sections of this great river are more than 11km (7 miles) wide, but when the rains come, the river takes possession of swathes of rainforest and swells to more than 40km (25 miles) across.

Despite the fact that development and climate change have devastated this region in recent decades, this is still an area of abundance where, with food and space to spare, many animals have grown big and bold. It's here that you'll find huge spiders, monstrously large snakes, gigantic reptiles like the Amazon River turtle and, of course, the giant otter.

Over many millennia, these beautiful beasts have evolved to make the most of a semi-aquatic, riverside life. Their flexible bodies are torpedo-shaped, with webbed feet and a muscular tail, which makes them acrobatic swimmers. They can also close their ears and nose while underwater, and their fur is so dense that their skin does not get wet. Their hands and feet are remarkably dextrous, enabling them to catch and manipulate a wide range of slippery, aquatic foods. Their super-sensitive whiskers help them to detect tell-tale movements beneath the water. And strong teeth and powerful jaws make short work of 'armoured' delicacies, like crabs. The otters' great size does make finding suitable habitats difficult, but there are definite

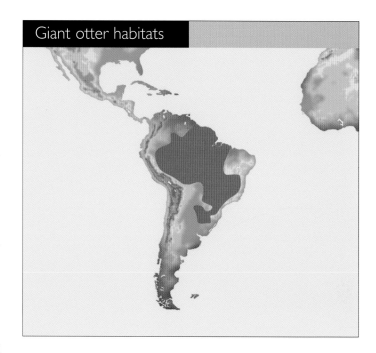

Giant otter habitats

advantages to being so bizarrely big, especially if it means that you're not restricted to a purely fish diet.

Family ties

They may look like over-sized dogs, but giant otters are one of the top predators in their environment. They have few natural enemies apart from man – who hunted it for its fur – and will tackle any animal not fast enough to escape their clutches. An adult giant otter needs to eat 6–10kg (13.2–22lb) of food per day. Most of their diet is medium-sized fish, but they've been known to eat catfish

Sliding his sleek body into the water with barely a ripple, the otter heads out to his favourite hunting site.

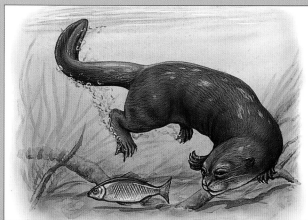

Propelled down, through the water, by his powerful tail and webbed feet, he soon spots a fish on the river bed.

weighing 20kg (44lb), herons, anacondas 9m (30ft) long and black caiman (*Melanosuchus niger*) more than 1.5m (4.9ft) long. One lone otter, even a giant one, would be unlikely to kill a caiman on its own, but otters have an advantage over other large, Amazonian predators. Though they do hunt alone, they also work together in pairs or even in groups.

Like many species of otters, these giants form tight-knit family bands containing two adults and several litters. Otter couples pair for life and family bonds are so strong that juveniles from previous litters will stay and tend new arrivals. Working together, the otter family makes a formidable foe and groups have been seen to call out, excitedly, to each other as they use their combined numbers to herd schools of fish into the shallows. It's when they come up against other predators like caiman, though, that these cooperative hunters are at their most impressive.

Giant otters are popular, playful and intelligent animals, whose looks have earned them the affectionate nickname 'water dogs'. However, they're also known as 'water wolves', for good reason. These animals are very territorial and surprisingly aggressive. They won't hesitate to band together to drive off intruders, especially species threatening their young. Ultimately, family ties, rather than their size, may hold the secret to their continued survival.

Comparisons

Sharing similar, semi-aquatic lifestyles means that all otters have a basic, streamlined body shape although their size varies from species to species. North American, northern river otters (*Lontra canadensis*) and African, spotted-necked otters (*Hydrictis maculicollis*) grow to about 1m (3.3ft) in length. That's half the size of giant otters. As shown in these images, there's also one, much subtler, difference between the species – the shape of their noses!

Spotted-necked otter

River otter

Giant otter

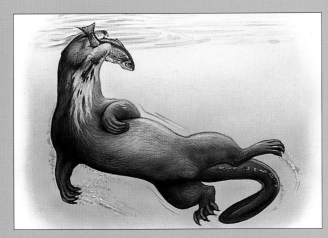

The fish may be fast and agile, but it is no match for the streamlined athleticism of a giant otter.

Retreating to a shady spot, the happy hunter eagerly devours his catch – crunching up the bones in his powerful jaws.

Hoatzin

Looking like some ancient archaeopteryx, the Hoatzin is one of the bird world's real oddities. It survives on a diet of wetland foliage and, because the food is so tough, it has developed a unique digestive system — more like a cow's than a bird's — to cope with it.

Juveniles
Young birds have wing claws, which they use to grip branches and climb back in to the nest if they fall out.

Crop

A food 'pouch' in the hoatzin's chest accounts for about 13 per cent of the bird's entire body weight.

Head

A small head supports an elaborate head crest. This crest gives the hoatzin its scientific name, *Opisthocomus hoazin,* meaning 'wearing long hair behind'.

Key Facts	ORDER *Cuculiformes* / FAMILY *Opisthocomidae* / GENUS & SPECIES *Opisthocomus hoazin*
Weight	Up to 816g (28.8oz)
Length	61–66cm (24–26in)
Sexual maturity	3 years
Breeding season	Rainy season
Number of eggs	2–5
Incubation period	28 days
Breeding interval	Once or twice a year
Typical diet	Fruit and leaves
Lifespan	Up to 8 years in the wild

With a dramatic, electric blue face, spiky head crest and trailing tail, hoatzins make a colourful addition to South America's tropical marshlands. These unusual birds make their homes in flooded forests along the banks of the Amazon and Orinoco river systems. It's a rich but challenging environment for any species to survive in but, over many millennia, these birds have adapted to make the best of life in and around these great wetlands.

Hoatzins breed when the river is at its height and food is plentiful, during the rainy season. Then, they build a stick nest on branches overhanging the flooded river banks. This means, if trouble strikes, chicks are able to head straight for water. They're excellent swimmers and come equipped with wing claws, which make it easier for them to climb

back to the nest once danger has passed. While their chicks are initially fed regurgitated food, pre-digested by the adult to make it easier to swallow, adults themselves enjoy the rich pickings that life in a river delta offers. They are known to eat at least 50 different species of plant and include fruit and flowers as well as leaves in their diet.

These marshland marvels are poor fliers, with 'reduced' wings, but have become adept at clambering through the foliage where young green leaves sprout. To help them scramble about on branches, they have a leathery bump on the bottom of their crop, which aids balance. Their long, showy tail adds much-needed stability. Such specialization has its drawbacks, though. It limits the hoatzins' range and, like many Amazonian species, these characterful birds are

An adventurous hoatzin chick sets out to explore, using its unique wing claws to keep a firm grip on vegetation.

Spotting danger ahead, the alarmed chick releases its grip and quickly drops down to the safety of the river below.

Using its feet and wings to paddle through the water, the hoatzin escapes. Hopefully the snake won't follow!

Keeping a wary watch for predators, the chick emerges from the water. If all's clear, he'll clamber back to the nest.

Hoatzin habitats

struggling to survive as their habitats are gradually lost to development.

The stink bird!

The hoatzins' scientific name, *Opisthocomus hoazin,* comes from the Greek for 'wearing long hair behind', a reference to its crest. The word hoatzin is said to be an onomatopoeic attempt to mimic the bird's distinctive, coarse call. However, these beautiful birds have another name – just as descriptive as their scientific and common names – but not nearly as flattering. They're known as stink birds!

The reason they've earned such an appalling appellation is due to their strange digestive system. For birds, digestion starts at the bill. This specialist tool is used for breaking open and grinding up food, and it eliminates the need for teeth. Once food has been cracked and crushed, it travels down to the crop, which is a muscular pouch in the throat. Most birds have a crop and it's used both to soften food and to regulate how quickly it moves on to the gizzard. This enables birds to gorge themselves when food is plentiful and store any 'excess' for later. Once food reaches the gizzard (really a specialized stomach), muscles grind it up. Some birds swallow stones, using them to help this process along.

What makes hoatzins so curious is that their crop is huge. In fact, it is so big that their flight muscles have been reduced to make space for it. It's here that much of the hoatzins' meal is broken down, but not in the usual way. Uniquely for birds, hoatzins use bacterial fermentation, like cattle, to digest their food. In cows, this process takes place in a special chamber called the rumen (which is why cattle are called ruminants). Hoatzins don't have this, so fermentation takes place in the crop. All this produces a distinctive farmyard odour. Put simply, hoatzin smell like manure!

Comparisons

Archaeopteryx lived during the Late Jurassic Period, 61–145 million years ago, in what would be modern-day Germany. The earliest undisputed hoatzin fossil dates from the Miocene, 23.03–5.33 million years ago, and was found in Colombia. While hoatzins do look strangely primitive, the two species are not related, although they share some physical traits, such as the chicks' wing claws and a similar skeletal structure.

Archaeopteryx   Hoatzin

Surinam Toad

These unusual amphibians are true ambush specialists. With their superb cryptic camouflage, they can hide in plain view, looking just like floating leaves, until prey passes within reach of their strange, star-shaped fingers. However, it's the toads' bizarre breeding habits that make them really remarkable.

Key Facts	ORDER *Anura* / FAMILY *Pipidae* / GENUS & SPECIES *Pipa species*
Weight	Up to 169g (6oz)
Length	Up to 18cm (7.1in)
Sexual maturity	3 years for Pipa pipa
Spawning season	Varies with species and location
Number of eggs	Up to 100
Incubation period	12–20 weeks, depending on species
Breeding interval	Yearly
Typical diet	Small invertebrates and fish
Lifespan	Up to 8 years in the wild, depending on species

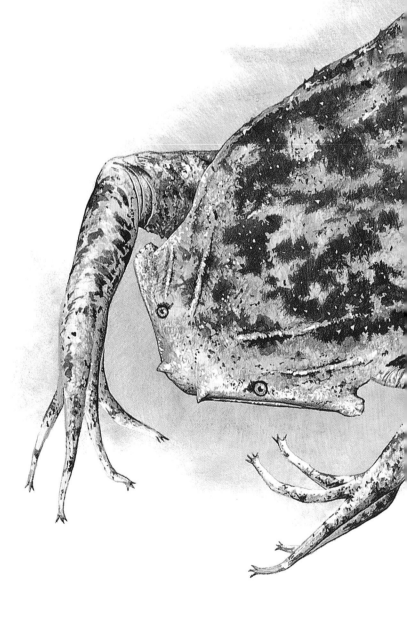

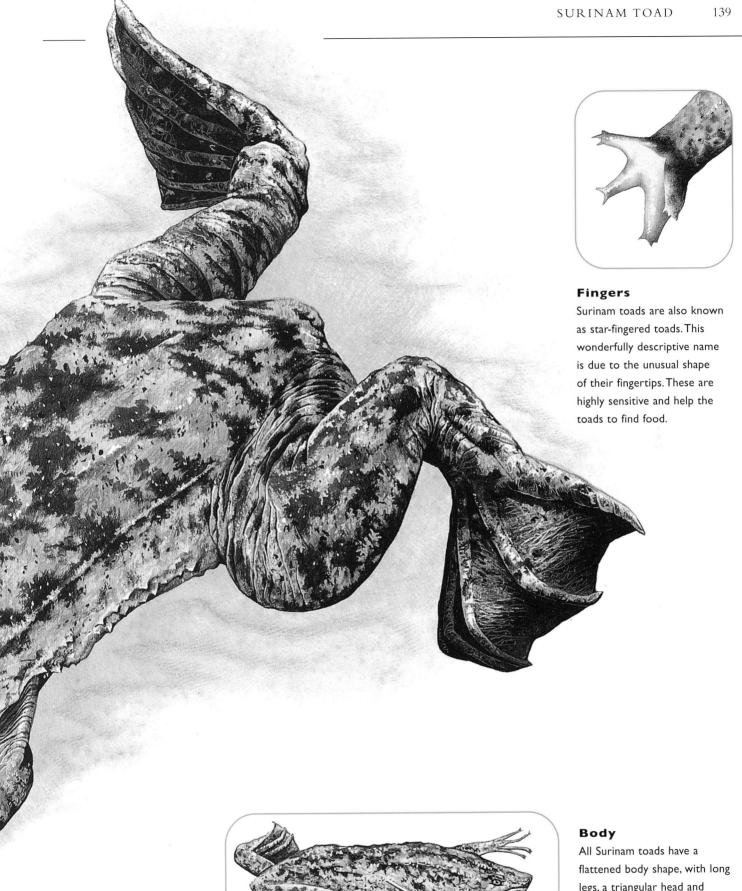

Fingers

Surinam toads are also known as star-fingered toads. This wonderfully descriptive name is due to the unusual shape of their fingertips. These are highly sensitive and help the toads to find food.

Body

All Surinam toads have a flattened body shape, with long legs, a triangular head and broadly webbed feet. They are usually a mottled green-brown colour resembling dead leaves.

Comparisons

African clawed frogs (*Xenopus laevis*) are a species of amphibian famous for their conspicuous black claws, which are used to grasp prey. These large frogs belong to the same family Pipidae as the Surinam toad and they share many traits – they're tongue-less, toothless and have almost aquatic lifestyles. Xenopus frogs are found in sub-Saharan Africa, while Surinam toads come from South America and Trinidad.

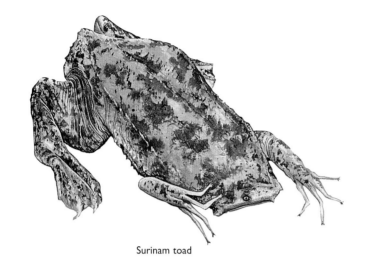

Surinam toad

African clawed frog

The word amphibian comes from the Greek *amphibios* meaning 'both kinds of life', which tells us that these incredible creatures can live both in water and on land. Frogs and toads of the family *Pipidae* are truly unusual amphibians in that they are mainly aquatic, and are rarely seen outside their watery homes. In fact, their favourite habitats are South America's slow, heavily silted streams and rivers. It's due to such an aquatic lifestyle that they have lost many of the physical characteristics we typically associate with frogs and toads.

Most members of the order *Anura*, to which frogs and toads belong, are bulky, full-bellied beasts, with long, powerful hind legs and elongated, flexible tongues, which they use to catch prey. By contrast, pipids have flattened, leaflike bodies. Combined with their mottled brown coloration, this makes for wonderfully effective cryptic camouflage, which helps these small amphibians to blend in with their surroundings. Pipids do have long legs, but their feet are completely webbed, suiting their aquatic lifestyles.

Frogs and toads are also famous for their noisy croaks and bellows, but Surinam toads have no vocal cords. They're not 'mute' but instead communicate in a rather strange way. They use bony rods in the larynx (voice box) to create clicks that help to attract a mate. In place of the usual long, sticky tongue, these peculiar amphibians have developed highly sensitive and mobile 'fingers'. Their usual hunting technique is to lie still, with their arms outstretched until they sense motion nearby. Then, they strike out, grabbing any passing prey, and pushing it into their wide mouths with a speedy, shovelling motion. Pipids are 'opportunistic' feeders and will make a meal of anything, from insects to fish.

Remarkable reproduction

Amphibians, like insects, have a complex life cycle, which involves a series of dramatic physical changes known as a metamorphosis.

Surinam toad habitats

During the mating season, common Surinam toads like to get up close and personal, but it's an acrobatic affair!

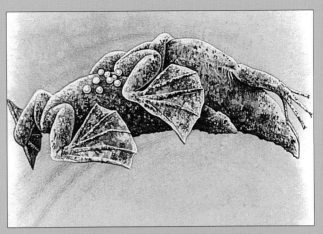

As the toads reach the top of an aquatic loop-the-loop, the female lays her eggs on the male's belly.

On the next loop, the male fertilizes the eggs and rubs them onto the female's back (on the brood patch).

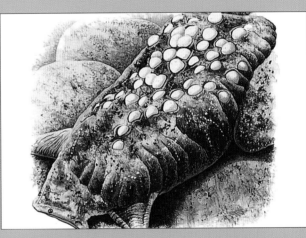

Several more somersaults leave the female's back festooned with eggs – and there they stay until ready to hatch.

For most frogs and toads, this whole remarkable process begins with a tiny cluster of eggs, floating, in a protective 'jelly'. Typically, eggs can be laid anywhere moist, but those deposited in water are often left to develop with no adult help. From here, they progress to the larval, tadpole stage. At this point, the immature frogs and toads are completely aquatic and look more like a fish than amphibians. They even have gills and a tail. Depending on the species, it takes from a few weeks to a few years for the tadpole to develop into a fully mature adult, which is when they tend to move on to land. These changes are more than just external. These amazing amphibians change internally too. Their skeletons are modified, lungs develop and their digestive tract is adapted to suit an adult, meat-eating diet, rather than the vegetarian diet they consumed as juveniles.

Not surprisingly, for such strange creatures, pipids have their own unique 'take' on the traditional amphibian metamorphosis. Eggs are laid on the females' back and sink into the spongy skin of her brood pouch. There they remain, in a series of honeycomb cells, until they are ready to hatch. In some species, the young emerge as tadpoles and finish their development in the water. In species such as *Pipa pipa* (the common Surinam toad) they emerge as fully grown toadlets, missing out the larval stage entirely. Such a remarkable reproductive cycle may seem odd, but it ensures that the toads are more likely to survive to adulthood.

Pygmy Marmoset

Looking like lions that have been magically miniaturized, pygmy marmosets are one of the New World's most surprising species of monkey. These ring-tailed rainforest inhabitants survive almost entirely on a diet of gum and sticky tree sap, which they tap using specialized incisor teeth.

Claws

Most primates have nails. This allows for the development of sensitive finger tips and manual dexterity. Although marmosets are primates, they have claws on all their digits except the big toe.

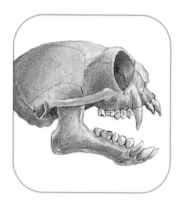

Teeth

Tree sap is one of the marmosets' favourite foods. Specialized incisor teeth at the front of the jaw help them to access the gum by gouging holes through thick bark.

Key Facts

ORDER *Primates* / **FAMILY** *Callitrichidae* / **GENUS & SPECIES** *Cebuella pygmaea*

Weight	113–199g (4–7oz)
Length	Up to 15cm (5.9in) Tail: up to 20cm (7.9 in)
Sexual maturity	18 months
Breeding season	All year
Number of young	2
Gestation period	4.5 months
Breeding interval	5–6 months
Typical diet	Sap, gum and insects
Lifespan	Up to 12 years in the wild; 20 in captivity

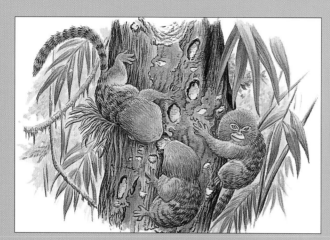

Breakfast is a popular time for these tiny primates and on the menu are exudates – tree sap and gum.

They say that a change is as good as a rest, and that's certainly true for these hungry little monkeys.

As the day moves on, marmosets switch to eating insects, using their long fingers to pluck them from the undergrowth.

Night falls, but before they retire for the night, the industrious marmosets gouge out some fresh sap holes, ready for breakfast.

When you're no bigger than the size of a tin of soup, it can be hard to compete with large rainforest species for food. Luckily, pygmy marmosets have evolved to take advantage of a very specialized environmental niche. They are gumophores.

These tiny monkeys have enlarged, forwards-turned, lower incisors, which grow to the same length as their canines. The lower set has no hard enamel on the inner surface, which makes them self-sharpening. This enables the marmosets to gouge holes through tree bark and make a meal of the sap or gum (called exudates), which is released. It's a tricky process, but the monkeys' long fingers and sharp claws help them to cling to the tree trunk while their teeth do the real work. As it takes some time for sap

to start flowing, it's estimated that around 67 per cent of the marmosets' day is spent feeding from pre-prepared holes or opening up new ones for later use.

To stay well fed, an average-sized marmoset troop, consisting of a breeding pair plus their offspring from the last two years, needs about 10.2–40.7 hectares (25–100 acres) of territory. This they actively defend, using calls, displays and scent marking, backed up by the occasional aggressive pursuits of intruders.

Tree sap isn't very nutritious, so the marmosets' sticky diet is supplemented with a regular intake of insects, insect larvae, small lizards, spiders and fruit. When it comes to hunting, being small is a positive advantage, and these furry fellows make surprisingly proficient predators. Their cryptic coloration, combined with catlike stealth and sudden, unexpected bursts of speed, enable them to catch even the most alert insects unaware.

Little lions

With their strikingly grizzled fur, long manelike head and chest hair and four-legged stance, these curious mammals are, not surprisingly, known in their homeland as *leoncito* – 'little lions'. Despite their convincingly leonine appearance, pygmy marmosets really are primates. In fact, they are one of the world's smallest primates and the smallest species of true monkey, which is why another nickname for them is *mono de bolsillo* – pocket monkey. (The smallest primate is the pygmy mouse lemur, *Microcebus myoxinus*.)

Monkeys and apes share many physical features, but there are also notable differences between the two groups. Monkeys have tails, but apes don't. Monkeys tend to move about on all fours using their tails for added grip and balance amongst the foliage. In the trees tops, apes brachiate (swing from branch to branch) or may clamber about on all fours. But they can and do walk on two legs, holding their bodies in an upright position, which makes them seem more human than their monkey cousins.

Scientifically speaking, marmosets are classed as New World monkeys as opposed to the Old World monkeys of Asia and Africa. Like all New World monkeys, they differ slightly from their Asian and African relations. The two most obvious differences come at either end of their

Pygmy marmoset habitats

bodies. New World monkeys are usually described as flat nosed, with nostrils to the side rather than facing forwards. They also tend to have prehensile (grasping) tails although marmosets, like tamarins, lack this adaptation. Instead, their tails are used like rudders to help them balance as they run through the tree tops. Marmosets are also unusual in that they don't have opposable thumbs but instead rely on sharp claws to help them to grip tree trunks.

Comparisons

Like pygmy marmosets, pied tamarins (*Saquinus bicolor*) are so tiny that they can be held in your hand. While pygmy marmosets live mainly on a diet of gum and sap, tamarins are frugivores. They mainly eat fruit and flowers, although they are known to occasionally consume small invertebrates. These beautiful primates get their name from their two-tone (pied) coat of white and reddish-brown fur.

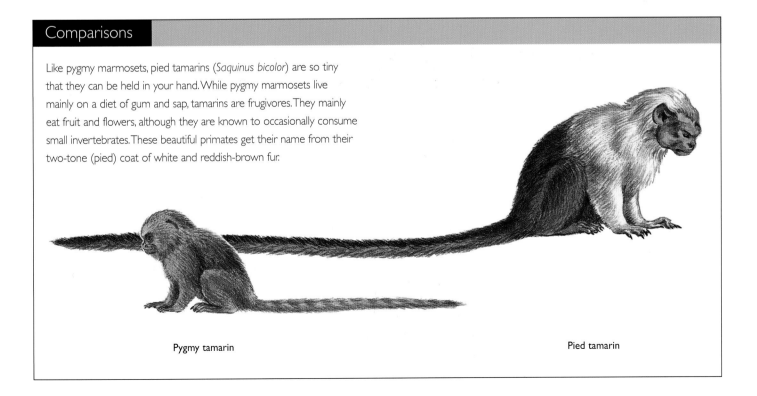

Pygmy tamarin   Pied tamarin

Red Howler Monkey

Howler monkeys are the Amazon Basin's very own nuisance neighbours. These stub-nosed primates make their homes in cloud forests, woods and mangrove swamps. They're creatures that like life in the tree tops, but being out of view doesn't mean that they're necessarily out of earshot!

Key Facts	ORDER *Primates* / FAMILY *Cebidae* / GENUS & SPECIES *Alouatta seniculus*	
Weight	Males: 5.4–9kg (11.9–19.8 lb) Females: 4.2–7kg (9.2–15.4lb)	
Length	Males: 49–72cm (19.3–28.3in) Females: 46–57cm (18.1–22.4in) Tail: 49–75cm (19.3–29.5 in)	
Sexual maturity	Males: 5–6 years. Females: 4–5 years	
Breeding season	All year	
Number of young	1	
Gestation period	190 days	
Breeding interval	Approximately 17 months	
Typical diet	Leaves, fruit and flowers	
Lifespan	Up to 20 years in the wild	

Hands

Long, flexible fingers are ideal for an arboreal, tree-dwelling lifestyle. The red howlers' thumbs are opposable and can be bent to touch the other digits. This gives them a superb grip.

Tail

Red howler monkeys have a powerful, prehensile (gripping) tail, which is strong enough to support their body weight. The underside of the tail lacks fur to give a better grip.

A tasty treat hanging on another branch proves to be too much of a temptation for this young howler monkey.

With a sudden crack, the branch beneath his feet breaks and the hungry howler begins to tumble down, towards ground.

No matter how many strange and spectacular animals a visitor to the Amazon might encounter, nothing is likely to prepare them for a howler monkey 'dawn chorus'! These rich, red-brown monkeys are the loudest animals in South America and the noises they produce can be truly startling.

It's generally the males that begin the famous howling chorus, using their eerie cries to declare their ownership of territory. Typically, one male begins and the rest of the troop joins in. Then, other troops, within earshot, reply, until the forest is jangling with raucous hoots and howls. It might not sound very sociable, but it's important 'work'.

The howlers' are folivores, so their diet is made up mostly of leaves. These aren't very nutritious, so every troop needs a big territory and a way to defend it without having to use too much energy. Since the best way to do this is by avoiding a fight in the first place, the howler monkeys use their voice. By calling out at the start and, sometimes, at the end of every day, they lay claim to their territory and prevent conflicts with any troop that might accidentally wander into it.

The howlers' cries are so loud that their roars can be heard up to 5km (3.1 miles) away. This is possible because they possess an enlarged lower jaw and an over-developed hyoid bone. This is the bone to which muscles from the floor of the mouth and the tongue are attached, and it acts a little like a loud speaker. By forming their mouths into tubes, howlers can produce a range of vibrant 'yodels' of varying intensity and length.

Interestingly, in reserves and zoos, howlers are less likely to make such a racket. Once they learn that there are no rivals in their local area, then they have much less to shout about.

Bad dads?

Howlers may be famous for their loud calls, but these rainforest-dwellers have a stranger – and bloodier – claim to fame.

Red howler troops are made up of several males and females and their offspring. Juvenile males are generally ejected from the troop once they reach sexual maturity and they may form their own, larger 'bachelor troops'.

Red howler monkey habitats

The monkey's long tail lashes out. Latching onto a strong branch, the howler takes advantage of this good fortune.

Disaster is averted – and a valuable lesson learnt. From now on, the howler will know to attach a 'safety line'!

Rivalry between males is intense, but only one male will become dominant and win the right to lead the troop and mate with the females. The dominant male must spend a great deal of time and energy defending his status. If he's thrown out of his own troop, it's likely that he won't be the only one to suffer.

The new male will often kill their rival's offspring as soon as he takes control of the troop. This has two effects. It brings the females into oestrus, which makes them sexually receptive so that he can mate with them. It also ensures that his unique genes are passed on to the next generation and that he doesn't spend time, energy and resources raising and protecting another male's offspring! This is such a widespread practice that it's estimated that less than one-quarter of red howler monkey infants survive the arrival of a new troop leader.

It's unpleasant to imagine that intelligent mammals like primates might indulge in such behaviour, but it's important to remember that they're just following their instincts – and these instincts tell them to stay alive and reproduce. Infanticide is simply the best strategy for the new, dominant male.

Comparisons

The dramatic, white-faced saki monkey (*Pithecia pithecia*) is another of the Amazon Basin's primate residents. While sakis form devoted couples who mate for life, red howler troops are polygynous, meaning that one male attempts to dominate the troop and breed with all the females. Adult sakis are also much smaller than their howler neighbours, at around 1.7-2kg (3.7–4.4lb), with non-prehensile, bushy tails.

White-faced saki monkey   Red howler monkey

Southern Tamandua

When they are nestled in the canopy, like some long-snouted tree-bear, it's hard to believe that tamanduas are really anteaters. These curious beasts like nothing better than licking up insects using their tapered tongue and tubelike snout. But beware – these cute creatures have claws and know to use them, too!

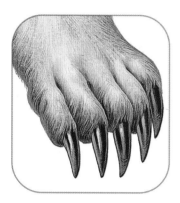

Feet

The tamanduas' feet are equipped with long, curved claws. Those on the mammals' hind feet are generally shorter then those on the fore feet, but they still make effective clamps to keep these arboreal-dwellers anchored in the tree tops.

Key Facts	ORDER *Xenarthra* / FAMILY *Myrmecophagidae* / GENUS & SPECIES *Tamandua tetradactyla*	
Weight	3–7kg (6.6–15.4 lb)	
Length	Up to 88cm (34.6in) Tail: 40–67cm (15.7–26.4 in)	
Sexual maturity	Females: 1 year	
Breeding season	Autumn	
Number of young	1	
Gestation period	130–160 days	
Breeding interval	Yearly	
Typical diet	Ants and termites	
Lifespan	Up to 9 years in captivity	

Tongue

A long, sticky tongue is used to lap up ants as they swarm to defend their home from the invading tamanduas.

There are currently more than 12,000 known species of ant. These industrious insects can be found on every continent except Antarctica and almost every country has its own, native species. Ants are equally at home in rainforests and deserts, and an average ant colony may contain several million individuals. Termites, too, are an amazingly widespread group. About 2750 species have been identified and, although they are never found more then 50° to the north or south of the Equator, they are

found in huge numbers. No wonder then, that so many animals take advantage of such a plentiful and nutritious food source.

There are four mammal species belonging to the suborder *Vermilingua* which eat ants and termites – the giant anteater *(Myrmecophaga tridactyla)*, the silky anteater *(Cyclopes didactylus)*, the southern tamandua (known as the collared anteater) and the northern tamandua *(Tamandua mexicana)*. The name anteater is also applied to aardvarks and pangolins, which are found in Africa and Asia, although they are not related to their South American counterparts.

Formicivorous mammals (those which feed mainly on ants) come in all shapes and sizes, but they share two vital adaptations to help them eat such small, speedy prey – powerful claws and a long, sticky tongue.

As their scientific name tells us (*tetradactyla* comes from the Greek for 'four-fingered'), tamanduas have four, clawed digits on their fore feet and five on their hind feet. It's their anterior (front) feet that they use to break open insect nests. Then, the tamanduas' tongue takes over. It is 40cm (15.7in) long, and the animals' enlarged salivary gland covers this tongue with sticky saliva, so all they have to do to enjoy a hearty feed is to lap the ants up.

At home and abroad

Tamanduas are arboreal, spending much of their time foraging for food amongst the tree canopy. Between 13 and 64 per cent of their day is spent in the tree tops and, for moving around in such a tricky environment, their

Tamanduas may enjoy a similar diet to the African aardvark, but their habitats couldn't be more different. These South American, furry 'ant-eaters' can be found in variety of environments, from tropical rainforest to savannah, but they spend most of their time in the trees. Africa's termite-munching aardvarks *(Orycteropus afer)* also enjoy a range of habitats but spend much of their day in underground burrows.

African aardvark

Southern tamandua

After enjoying a quick, mid-morning snack of ants, the tamandua shuffles back towards the safety of the nearest tree.

Before he can clamber back up, he notices trouble heading his way. It's an inquisitive coati – and he doesn't look friendly.

Appearances can be deceptive. This tamandua is no pushover! Backing against the tree trunk, he gets ready for a fight.

As the coati moves in, the tamandua lashes out with his sickle-shaped claws, leaving the intruder bloodied and bruised.

long, curved claws are invaluable. These act like a mountaineer's crampons, anchoring them to branches and enabling them to haul themselves up and down tree trunks with ease. They also have a prehensile (gripping) tail that works like an additional limb. This can be wrapped around branches for support as they climb. Their weight means they're restricted to thicker branches, but they are remarkably agile amongst the foliage. Once tamanduas are on the ground, though, it's a different story.

To avoid puncturing their palms with their sharp claws, tamanduas walk on the outsides of their feet, which produces a slow, waddling gait. Despite this, they often have large territories, especially in scrubland areas where food is less plentiful.

Naturally solitary by nature, each tamandua forages alone but, because these animals are so slow on the ground, they are vulnerable to attack. However, their claws and tail – which are so useful in the tree tops – also provide them with the means to defend themselves on the forest floor. When aggravated, tamanduas hiss and release an unpleasant scent, which has earned them the nickname 'stinkers of the forest'! If that doesn't do the trick, then they back up against a tree trunk or rock. Rearing up on their hind legs, they use their tails, like a tripod, for support, making their fore legs available for wrestling and leaving their front claws free to lash out. One slash from those formidable talons is enough to scare away most predators.

Three-toed Sloth

These famous somnambulists spend an average of 10 hours a day snoozing, which has earned them the nickname *bicho-preguiça* (lazy animal). When they do wake up, they spend so much time simply hanging around that their bodies are adapted to a life spent upside-down!

Key Facts	ORDER *Edentata* / FAMILY *Bradypodidae* / GENUS & SPECIES *Bradypus genus*	
Weight	3.5–4.5kg (7.7–9.9lb)	
Length	56–60cm (22–23.6in) Tail: 6–7cm (2.4–2.5 in)	
Sexual maturity	3–4 years, but depends on species	
Breeding season	March–April, but depends on species	
Number of young	1	
Gestation period	6 months	
Breeding interval	1–2 years, but depends on species	
Typical diet	Leaves and buds	
Lifespan	Up to 12 years in the wild; 20 in captivity	

Claws

Three toes on each foot are tipped with hooked claws. These are so strong that sloths can hang from them.

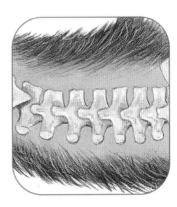

Spine

Regardless of their shape or size, most mammals, even long-necked giraffes, have seven cervical vertebrae (neck bones). Two-toed sloths have only six cervical vertebrae, but three-toed sloths have nine. This enables them to look forwards while hanging upside-down.

Sloths are such famously slow-moving animals that their name is a byword for laziness. Yet the truth is that these lethargic creatures aren't really lazy at all. They're just superbly energy-efficient.

Sloths are folivores, which means that the bulk of their diet consists of leaves and buds. This isn't an especially nutritious or energy-rich food source, so sloths have enlarged stomachs with multiple compartments. These compartments contain cellulose-digesting bacteria that help break down the tough fibres. Around two-thirds of the weight of a well-fed sloth consists of the contents of their stomach, and their metabolisms are so slow they can take up to one month to completely digest a meal. Even then, they get so little fuel from the food they eat that

they need to be extremely energy-efficient in their habits. This is why sloths move as little as possible and leave the tree tops only once a week to defecate!

They spend hours grazing in ultra-slow motion and, after filling their bellies, sloths will settle down to sleep for at least 10 hours each day. Their bodies are pared down to an energy-efficient minimum. It takes a lot of food energy to build and maintain muscle, so sloths make do with less than half the muscle mass of other mammals. They are warm-blooded, but because they convert food into energy at half the rate of a similar-sized mammal they have difficulty retaining a high or constant body temperature. Instead, they warm themselves by snoozing in selected sunny spots. If temperatures fall, then they

Life in the rainforest can be dangerous. If predators don't get you, flooding rivers may leave you marooned.

Sloths may be slow and lethargic, but they do have one surprising skill – they are strong and efficient swimmers.

Unfortunately, clambering back up on to dry land isn't that easy, and it's here that sloths are at their most vulnerable.

They can't walk so they must pull themselves along on all fours, which makes them a prime target for any predator.

curl into a ball, and rely on a special system of blood vessels to focus warmth around their vital organs, where it's most needed.

Topsy-turvy

Sloths can be found from Panama to northern Argentina, where they make their homes in the region's tropical rainforests. While many animals are well adapted to an arboreal lifestyle, sloths are such specialists that their bodies have become truly extraordinary.

Clambering about in the tree tops is tiring and so, to save energy, sloths eat, mate, give birth and nurse their young dangling, upside down, from a convenient branch. In fact, they have difficulty supporting their weight in an upright position, and must spend much of their time simply hanging around. They are able to do this thanks to a flexible spine, long limbs and a set of remarkably strong, curved claws. These claws make such efficient grappling hooks that dead sloths are difficult to dislodge from their branches! The result of such a topsy-turvy lifestyle has been that the position of many of the sloths' internal organs is different from those of other mammals. Even their hair grows downwards, from their stomach towards their back, so that rain water flows off when they're upside down.

Despite their infamous lack of speed, life in the tree tops is surprisingly safe for a sloth, thanks to their natural caution and camouflage. They rarely leave the safety of the foliage and have even been known to urinate during

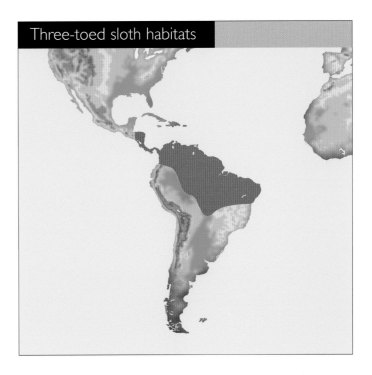

Three-toed sloth habitats

rainstorms to avoid drawing attention to themselves. Their long, gray-brown hair blends in so well with the surrounding environment that when they curl into a ball to sleep they can easily be mistaken for a termite nest or a knot of vegetation. During the rainy season, this fur even takes on a coat of blue-green algae (species *Trichophilius* and *Cyanoderma*), which provides additional cryptic camouflage.

Comparisons

Although they look similar and occupy roughly the same geographic range, it's believed that two- and three-toed sloths (species *Choloepus*) aren't closely related. Two-toed sloths are probably descended from the giant, extinct ground sloths that once dominated South America's rainforests. Thanks to a much wider diet (which includes small vertebrates), the two-toed sloth are generally larger and faster than the three-toed variety.

Two-toed sloth

Three-toed sloth

NORTH
SEA

NORTH
ATLANTIC
OCEAN

Scandinavia

EUROPE

Alps

Massif
Central

Apehnines

BLACK
SEA

MEDITERRANEAN
SEA

North Africa

Europe

Europe is the world's second-smallest continent. Home to about
731 million people, this tightly packed landmass stretches across
14 time zones from Iceland, in the heart of the grey, wind-blown
Atlantic Ocean, to the sweeping expanse of the Russian steppes.

~

People have inhabited this continent for thousands of years, and both flora and fauna have been profoundly affected. There are few true wilderness areas left. This is a continent that was once almost completely covered by forest, but much of this has now been cut down. In recent years, attempts have been made to restore some of this habitat, or at least to maintain what is left.

And yet, Europe is one of the most cosmopolitan of continents. Here we find bare Norwegian tundra, temperate British woodlands, lush French vineyards, parched Iberian plains, scented Alpine meadows, mountains, valleys and coral reefs.

Not surprisingly, such diverse habitats are home to a stunning variety of wildlife. Europe doesn't have the space to support the vast numbers of animals that regularly rumble across the African plains. Nor does it have acres of unexplored rainforest where such species as those found in South America can grow big and bold without the interference of man. There are no great deserts, or thundering rivers within this crowded and compact continent, but it still has its share of wonderful, wild spaces and islands of green, where wildlife – in all its strange and surprising forms – can flourish.

Compass Jellyfish

These shapeless blobs are every bit as odd as anything that a writer of science fiction might conjure up. Their bodies are more than 90 per cent water, with no circulatory system, respiratory system or brain, but it's when they mate that things really get weird.

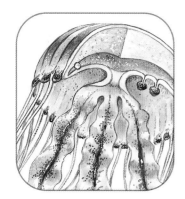

Body

These jellyfish get their name from the V-shaped markings and dark circles on their bells, which resemble an old-fashioned mariner's compass.

Key Facts	ORDER *Semaeostome* / FAMILY *Ulmaridae* GENUS & SPECIES *Chrysaora hysoscella*	
Length of tentacles	Up to 60cm (23.6in)	
Diameter of bell	20–30cm (7.9–11.8in)	
Sexual maturity	Not recorded	
Planulae released	Spring, depending on conditions	
Number of young	Not recorded	
Time from larvae to adult	2–3 years, depending on conditions	
Breeding interval	Varies, depending on conditions	
Typical diet	Small planktonic animals and fish	
Lifespan	Up to 6 months as an adult	

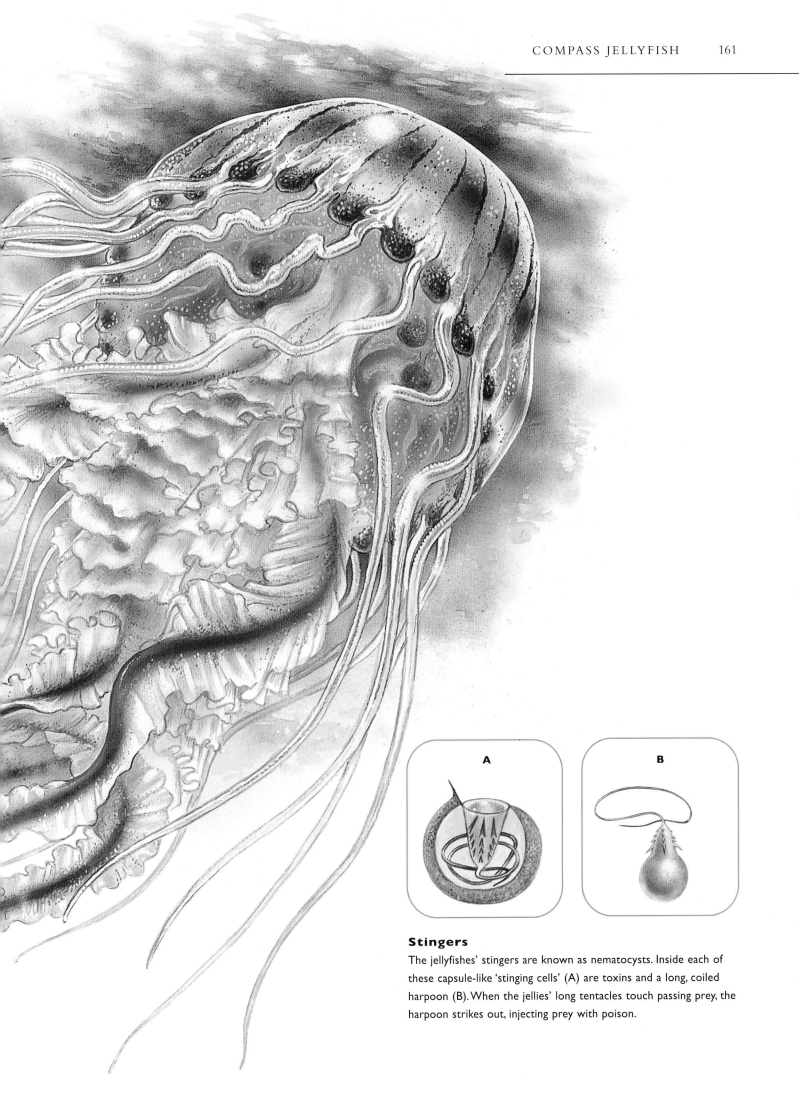

Stingers

The jellyfishes' stingers are known as nematocysts. Inside each of these capsule-like 'stinging cells' (A) are toxins and a long, coiled harpoon (B). When the jellies' long tentacles touch passing prey, the harpoon strikes out, injecting prey with poison.

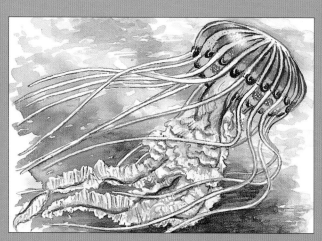

Jellyfish reproduction is far from straightforward, although it begins, naturally enough, with the male's sperm fertilizing the female's eggs.

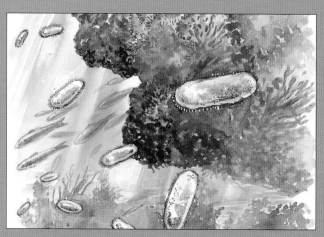

After fertilization has taken place, the female releases tiny larvae, known as planulae, which come to rest in shallow water.

In the world of jellies, mating isn't merely a matter of boy meets girl. It's more a case of boy becomes girl! Scientifically speaking, adult compass jellyfish are considered to be protandrous sequential hermaphrodites, which means that they function initially as males and then, later in their lives, become females. It sounds curious, but this does have its advantages.

Compass jellyfish habitats

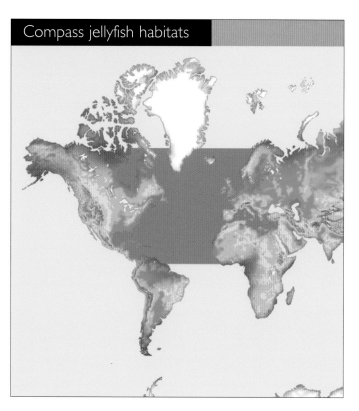

When you spend your life roaming the oceans, it can be hard to find a partner, but luckily compasses don't need to meet to mate. Males simply release their sperm into the water and this fertilizes any suitable eggs it encounters. Fertilization takes place inside the female and she releases free-swimming larvae (known as planulae) during the summer or autumn. Planulae are tiny, with flattened bodies in which both halves are mirror images – a condition known as bilateral symmetry.

These 'jelly babies' settle onto the sea bed or attach themselves to any safe, secluded surface. There, within a few days, they develop into scyphistoma. In this form, they are sessile – they are not able to move around – but rely on their tentacles to grab passing plankton in order to eat. Depending on how well they have fed, the scyphistoma may be ready to reproduce themselves by the following spring. The upper part of these marvellous creatures then divides to produce flower-shaped embryos (called ephyrae), which float away to begin lives of their own. This second-stage reproduction is asexual, as opposed to sexual reproduction, which involves the combination of male gametes, called sperm, and female gametes called eggs or ova.

These miniature jellyfish may take up to two years to develop into fully mature adults (known as medusas), and then the whole wonderfully strange process is ready to begin all over again.

Hydraulic hunters

Jellies don't waste energy chasing down prey. They let time and the tides do the job for them. This doesn't mean that

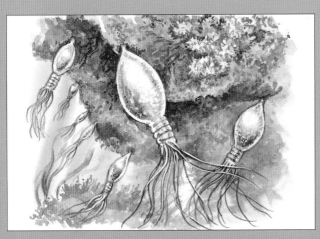

After anchoring themselves to a well-secluded piece of rock, the larvae develop into scyphistoma, which have tentacles for catching food.

Over time, the scyphistoma produce tiny jellyfish, just 5mm (0.2in) in diameter, and these quickly develop into mature jellyfish.

they're helpless creatures, flung from coast to coast by ocean currents. When they need to, they can swim by contracting and relaxing their bell in a series of rhythmic pulses, which pushes water out and propels them forwards. But, they're usually found floating free in the upper layers of coastal waters, where food is plentiful and all they have to do is wait for it brush past.

Compass jellyfish eat small fish, crustaceans and plankton and they do this using specialized stinging organs called nematocysts, which line the jellies' bell and their 24 marginal tentacles. Each nematocyst contains a coiled, threadlike tube lined with barbed spines. Inside these small 'capsules', the osmotic pressure (the difference between the pressure inside and out) is extremely high. When one of the jellyfishes' tentacles touches prey, the nematocyst is activated. Water rushes into the capsule, which increases hydrostatic pressure (the pressure exerted by a fluid). This, in turn, expels the barbed thread, like a harpoon being shot from a gun. The spine penetrates the prey's skin, injecting it with paralyzing poison.

Using this amazing system, small creatures can be caught and pulled into the mouth of the compass with little danger of their struggles damaging the delicate structure of the jelly's body. Nematocysts work equally well in defence too, giving would-be predators a stinging jolt. Although compass jellyfish aren't as poisonous as other species, their barbs are still extremely painful to people. Even a dead compass jellyfish, washed up on the shore, should be avoided because it is still capable of inflicting a painful sting.

Comparisons

In these images, compass and lion's mane jellyfish (*Cyanea capillata*) may look similar but, in real life, lion's manes are giants! In northern oceans they can grow to about 50cm (19.7in) in diameter, with tentacles up to 30m (98.4ft). The largest-ever recorded specimen had a bell of 2.3m (7.5ft) and tentacles of 36.5m (119.7ft) long!

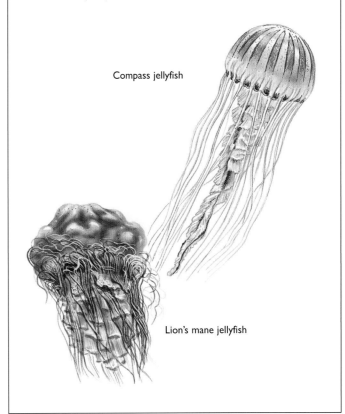

Compass jellyfish

Lion's mane jellyfish

Cuckoo

Cuckoos are well known for their mercenary method of parenting. While other birds struggle to raise their young, common cuckoos sit back and let others do the work for them. But don't judge these beautiful birds too harshly. Such strange behaviour is all down to instinct.

Key Facts	ORDER *Cuculiformes* / FAMILY *Cuculidae* GENUS & SPECIES *Cuculus canorus*
Weight	100–150g (3.5–5.3oz)
Length	55–65cm (21.6–25.6in) Wingspan: 32–34cm (12.6–13.4in)
Sexual maturity	1–2 years
Breeding season	Late May, but varies with location
Number of eggs	1–25
Incubation period	11–12 days
Breeding interval	Yearly
Typical diet	Insects
Lifespan	Up to 13 years

Legs & Feet

Cuckoos legs are short but strong. Their feet have a zygodactyl layout, with two of their toes pointing forwards and two pointing backwards. This is common for most perching birds, particularly those that spend their time climbing tree trunks or clambering through foliage such as woodpeckers or parrots. Such a design means that they walk with a hopping gait.

This cunning cuckoo sees no reason to raise her own young when plenty of other birds could do it for her!

Spotting a reed warbler nest she quickly moves in – removing one of the warbler's eggs and laying a replacement.

The cuckoo's chick hatches before the warbler's and then throws the remaining egg from the nest.

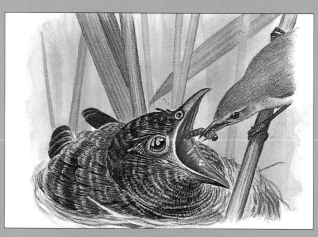

At just two weeks old, the warbler parents are already struggling to keep up with the massive chick's demands for food.

Why would a bird entrust its offspring to the care of another species? It seems like a risky business, but for some animals it's an extremely successful breeding strategy.

Cuckoo wasps and cuckoo bees both use a form of brood parasitism, where they lay their eggs in the nests of other insects. As these insect names tells us, though, it's cuckoos who are infamous for leaving others literally holding the baby.

Rearing a child is a time-consuming business that demands energy. Any species that can raise a big family with little effort is sure to be successful, and the common cuckoo manages this with ease. One female can produce as many as 25 young in a season – something she could never do by conventional means. Instead she carefully times her egg laying to coincide with that of the host species. To reduce the chances of discovery, she removes one host egg and lays one of her own in each nest. The switch takes just a few seconds.

Meadow pipits, dunnocks and reed warblers are commonly chosen as hosts. Eggs that resemble the hosts' are less likely to discovered and thrown out of the nest. So chicks raised by one species will always lay their eggs in nests belonging to the same species to ensure the best possible match.

Once hatched, the young cuckoo quickly disposes of its 'brothers' and 'sisters', by heaving the eggs or chicks out of the nest. This leaves the cuckoo free to gorge itself on all the food that its poor 'parents' can supply. Although the

Cuckoo habitats

is Eurasian, spending its summers in Europe and Asia and winters in Africa. In Britain, the arrival of the cuckoo is always welcomed as a sign that spring is on the way: readers of the *The Times* newspaper have been known to write in to report hearing the first characteristic 'cuk-oo' call, after which the bird is named.

In these temperate zones, cuckoos are primarily insectivores and will eat almost any insect. Their curved bills make short work of everything from spiders to beetles, but they seem to have a real taste for the unusual. The common cuckoo feeds on hairy, toxic caterpillars such as those of the cinnabar moth (*Tyria jacobaeae*), which most birds are careful to avoid.

Many caterpillar species are unpalatable due to the fact that their bodies absorb bitter-tasting alkalis from the plants they eat. At best, this makes them taste extremely unpleasant. At worst, it makes them poisonous. Many also have urticating (barbed) hairs, which embed themselves in the skin, eyes and soft parts of predators, or anyone else unlucky enough to stumble across them. *Urtica* is Latin for nettle and eating a hairy caterpillar is like munching down a bunch of stinging nettles!

Cuckoos, though, have developed a cunning technique for handling such tricky food. They bite off the heads of the caterpillars and then, before swallowing them, they shake them, presumably to expel their toxic innards. After this, it's a simple matter to swallow the remains – hair and all. Cuckoos periodically shed their stomach lining, depositing it as a neat pellet, which safely removes all of those irritating hairs.

cuckoo chicks look nothing like their own offspring, instinct compels the parents to continue feeding the impostors until they're big enough to fledge.

Curious cuisine

Cuckoos come can be found in both temperate and tropical regions. Many live in the rainforests of Australia, South America, Asia and Africa, but the common cuckoo

Comparisons

There's no doubt that common cuckoos have a bad reputation when it comes to their parenting techniques, but only around 40 per cent of all cuckoos are brood parasites. Other species have less dramatic ways of reproducing. Some build nests and raise their own young while others, like the black-billed cuckoo (*Coccyzus erythropthalmus*), lay eggs in other birds' nests only when food is plentiful.

Common cuckoo

Black-billed cuckoo

Death's Head Hawkmoth

Of the 1200 or so known species of hawkmoths, the death's head is probably
the most famous. Thanks to their strange 'death's head' skull pattern, they have a
reputation as harbingers of death. Yet, what really makes these creepy-looking
creatures so strange is their remarkable life cycle.

Pupa

The pupa is the hard casing
that protects the insects as
they undergo their
transformation from
caterpillars to adult moths.

Key Facts	ORDER *Lepidoptera* / FAMILY *Sphingidae* GENUS & SPECIES *Acherontia atropos*	
Weight	Adults: 7g (0.2oz)	
Length	Adults: 4–5cm (1.6–2in)	
Sexual maturity	1–2 months	
Breeding season	May–October	
Number of eggs	Up to 150	
Egg to ault	4–6 months	
Breeding interval	Adults die after mating	
Typical diet	Caterpillars: nightshade plants Adults: honey, sap and nectar	
Lifespan	Adults: 2–3 months	

Thorax

Skull markings on the thorax and skeletal stripes along the moths' body give these insects a distinctly creepy appearance.

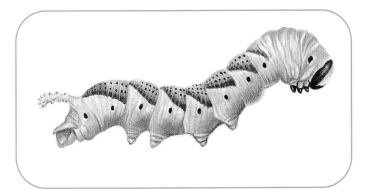

Caterpillar

Death's head caterpillars come in three colours – green, yellow-striped and brown. All have a curious bent horn at the tail-end.

Insects are so plentiful and commonplace that it's easy to forget just how strange they really are. Almost all insects have an amazingly complex life cycle. The more primitive, wingless species develop into adults by shedding their outer skins as they grow. Winged insects undergo a much more dramatic transformation, which entails either an incomplete or a complete metamorphosis.

The word metamorphosis comes from the Greek words *meta,* meaning change, and *morphe,* meaning form or shape. Remarkably, that's what every butterfly and every moth does, along with many other insect species – change shape. For such insects, early life is spent in a larval form. In the case of moths and butterflies, these larvae are known as caterpillars, and they're basically massive eating machines. They grow so quickly that they need to shed and replace their skin regularly to accommodate their growing bulk. It's only once they've stored up enough fuel to begin their amazing metamorphosis that they stop eating and pupate.

During the pupal stage, butterflies and moths cocoon themselves in a hard, protective shell. There they remain, immobile, while their bodies are gradually broken down and reformed. It's a staggeringly complex procedure but one which is so successful that 85 per cent of all insects develop into adulthood this way.

All of this energy and effort is for one purpose only – to reproduce. Males track females down by following the unique scent they leave behind, and once adult death's head moths have sniffed out a partner, the two mate and

Death's head hawkmoth habitats

then die. But what is really amazing about this whole cycle of birth, metamorphosis and death is that such a staggering feat of nature usually happens, completely unnoticed, in our own back gardens.

Power food

For the death's head moth – as for other members of the order *Lepidoptera* – the transformation from larvae to adult

Comparisons

The beautiful hummingbird hawkmoth (*Macroglossum stellatarum*) may not be as large as its infamous cousin, but it's just as widely travelled. Death's head moths can be found from Britain to the Cape of Good Hope, although they're very common in Africa and southern Asia. The hummingbird moth breeds much more widely and has been known to migrate as far as the United States and Polar regions.

Death's head hawkmoth   Hummingbird hawkmoth

The death's head hawkmoths has a short 'proboscis' (tubelike eating apparatus). This leaves it no choice: it must steal to live!

While other hawkmoths feed by sucking up nectar from flowers, the death's head robs beehives of their honey.

The moth's unusual death's-head coloration and the high-pitched squeaks it produces help to ensure that their break-ins are successful.

Worker bees confuse the moths' signals with those of their queen and won't attack — leaving the death's head free to gorge!

requires a complete change of diet and lifestyle. As adults, death's heads lose the powerful mandibles they once used to munch through greenery. In their place, they develop a tonguelike proboscis, which is designed to suck up honey. Fortunately, the moths' strange markings and the curious squeaks they make (by blowing air through the proboscis) enables them to steal all the honey they need from a hive. No one knows for sure, but these 'disguises' seem to confuse worker bees. It's believed that the bees mistake the moths for their own queen, which is why they don't attack when the intruders come looking for a sweet treat.

But why should death's head moths need such a rich source of energy when potato leaves previously provided them with enough fuel to transform from larvae to adult?

The answer is simple. Once they reach adulthood, these marvellous moths are in a race against the clock. They live for only a short period of time and must mate before they die to ensure that their unique genes are passed on to the next generation. Their newly developed wings help to speed up the search for a mate, and death's head moths use them to great effect. In fact, members of the hawkmoth family (*Sphingidae*) are some of the fastest moths in the world, reaching speeds of up to 48.3km/h (30mph) as they flit amongst the foliage. The only problem is that flying requires a lot of energy. Thankfully, there are fewer sources of food as calorie-rich as honey!

European Honey Bee

Honey bee society is not so much strange as surprising. We may imagine that the life of a worker bee is one of mindless drudgery, but these intelligent insects live in amazingly complex communities and communicate with each other in ways that scientists still struggle to understand.

Key Facts	ORDER *Hymenoptera* / FAMILY *Apidae* GENUS & SPECIES *Apis mellifera*
Length	Queen: up to 2cm (0.8in)
Length	Worker: up to 1.5cm (0.6in)
Length	Drone: up to 1.8cm (0.7in)
Eggs laid	Up to 1.5 million during Queen's life
Size of colony	40,000–80,000
Larval period	17–24 days
Group name	Swarm or colony
Typical diet	Nectar and pollen
Lifespan	Up to 6 years for Queen; 8 weeks for workers

Legs

The legs of honey bees are used for more than just walking. Super-sensitive, they enable the bees to detect, collect and 'pack' pollen, as well as carry out work in the hive. This is possible using specialized hairs on different parts of the legs. Those on the outer tibia of the hind legs, for instance, are especially long and act as 'pollen baskets'.

Comparisons

With their stout, hairy bodies, European honey bees are perhaps the most familiar members of the bee family. These hard-working insects share their range with many other species of bee, and while most of these are indistinguishable to all but the experts, they have very different lifestyles. Leafcutter bees (*Megachilidae species*) and bumblebees (*genus Bombus*), for instance, have much simpler social structures and correspondingly smaller colonies.

Honey bee

Bumblebee

Leafcutter bee

A honey bee colony is like a company. At its head is the Chief Executive Officer (CEO), who is literally the queen bee. Every hive has just one queen and while all the workers are female, the queen is the only female that's fertile and able to produce the next generation of bees. It's also the job of the queen to regulate the hive's activities by producing chemicals called pheromones, which guide the activities of the rest of the community. The workers are responsible for building and maintaining the nest, feeding and caring for the young and finding food.

Even though the CEO is the boss, the rest of the colony decides when a new queen is needed. This occurs either when an existing queen becomes ill or dies, or when the hive begins to run out of space. If the queen is ill, she'll be often be dispatched by the workers who then begin to feed one of the undeveloped larvae with royal jelly – a nutrient-rich food that turns otherwise sterile workers into fertile, potential queens. The first to hatch will generally fight it out for the top job, stinging their rivals to death!

If the colony is just too full, then the bees will swarm and the old queen will head off with around half of her workers to form a new 'franchise'. New queens will then be raised and the successful candidate will take on the business of the old hive. Choosing their new nest site is a

European honey bee habitats

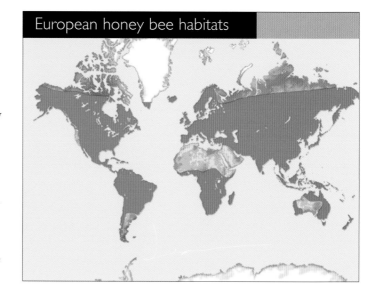

complex business and the bees handle it in a surprising way. They use a system called quorum sensing and, like bee society itself, it's amazingly sophisticated.

Building a franchise

A beehive may seem like it's dominated by the dictatorial queen, but the workers choose when and where to build a new hive.

Initially, small groups of workers will leave the swarm on scouting expeditions and then return to report news of their finds. They attract interest in their preferred site by using a form of waggle dance, which is also how workers communicate information about food to each other. The better the new site is, the more complex the dance is. Once the worker has a quorum interested in her site, the workers will then head off to recruit more supporters. Once enough of the swarm are convinced of the merits of the new site, they'll establish a new nest.

Now it's back to business as usual. The queen is installed in her new nest, and spends several days orienting herself. Then she leaves the beehive to mate with the male drones from several different hives, in order to fill her spermatheca, where male sperm is stored. She now has no need to mate again in order to reproduce, and can begin to lay eggs.

For the queen, egg-laying can be a year-long job, although it peaks in spring, when food is plentiful, and it may stop completely in winter. At the height of her egg laying, she may produce up to 2500 eggs a day.

The eggs that are fertilized will become workers. Those that are not will become drones. So the phrase 'as busy as a bee' is certainly accurate. These industrious insects never seem to stop. Workers born at the height of the hive's workload, may live for only around five weeks. Queens can survive for 5–6 years, but such a hectic life quickly wears them out.

It wasn't until 1973 that honey bee communication was revealed to the world, thanks to the work of ethologist Karl von Frisch (1886–1982).

Many did not believe him, but he was the first scientist to suggest that honey bees communicate by dancing! Here, a scout does a round dance to tell others where flowers are.

Round dances reveal the general location of food within 30m (98.4ft) If food is farther away, bees have developed a way to deliver more complex instructions.

The waggle dance gives precise directions. The angle of the dancer relates to the angle between the hive and Sun, and the speed of the dance indicates the distance.

Great Diving Beetle

These iridescent insects may look harmless but, in their own watery world, they're tigers! These pint-sized predators have voracious appetites and will attempt to eat anything they can catch using an in-built aqualung to help them dive into deep waters in pursuit of their prey.

Larvae
These large larvae look more like shrimp than beetles, especially with their 'tails' raised in the water to take in air.

Key Facts	ORDER *Coleoptera* / FAMILY *Dytiscidae* GENUS & SPECIES *Dytiscus marginalis*	
Weight	Not recorded	
Length of larvae	Up to 6cm (2.4in)	
Length of adult	Up to 4cm (1.5in)	
Sexual maturity	On reaching adult stage	
Spawning season	Spring and summer	
Breeding interval	Yearly	
Number of eggs	1000	
Typical diet	Shrimps, tadpoles and small fish	
Lifespan	Adults: up to 3 years in the wild	

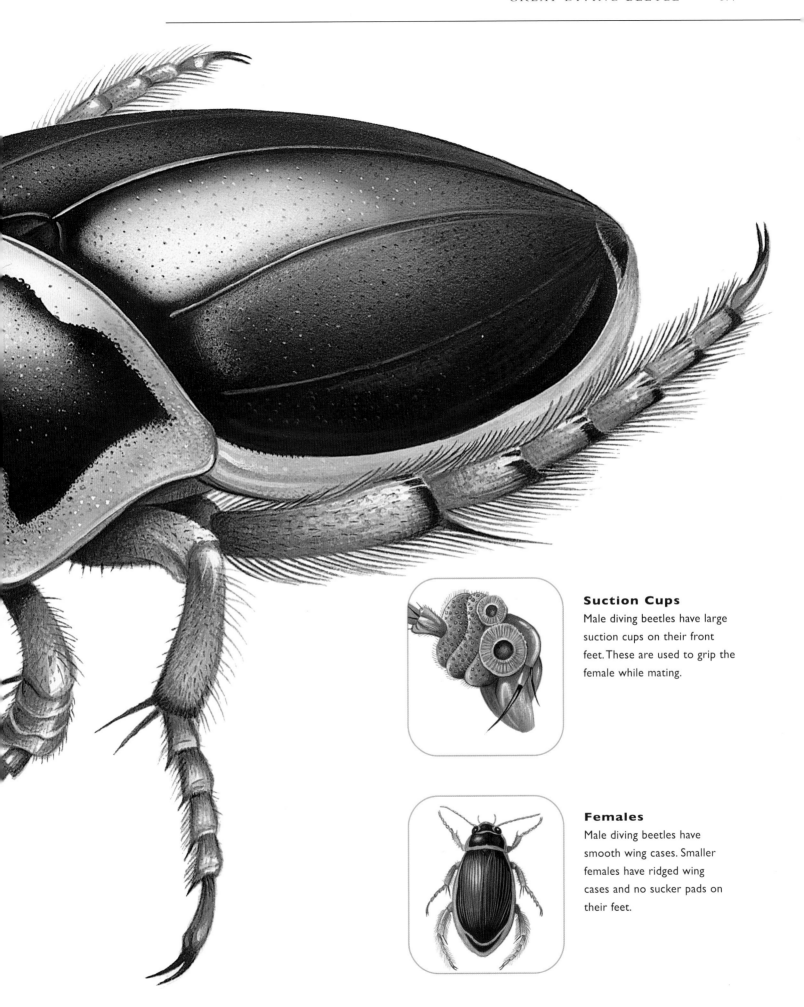

Suction Cups

Male diving beetles have large suction cups on their front feet. These are used to grip the female while mating.

Females

Male diving beetles have smooth wing cases. Smaller females have ridged wing cases and no sucker pads on their feet.

Comparisons

Despite their name, great silver water beetles *(Hydrophilus piceus)* are greenish-black not silver. Like their relatives, the great diving beetles, these are aquatic insects, who breathe underwater by trapping air bubbles in the hairs on the underside of their body, and the bubbles give them their silver sheen. Although larger than great diving beetles in size, these insects aren't predators but algae-loving herbivores.

Great diving beetle

Great silver water beetle

Around one out of every three insects is a beetle. There are an estimated 370,000 recognized species and these incredible creatures can be found in every part of the world apart from the oceans and the Poles. Although this diverse and hugely successful family varies enormously, diving beetles are perhaps one of the strangest members of the order *Coleoptera*, in that they're aquatic.

It's easy to think that all insects fall into just two distinct groups. The 'creepy crawlies' who spend their lives burrowing through the earth and the colourful 'fliers', like the moths, who brighten up our gardens. Many insects,

though, spend at least part of their life cycle in water, often in the immature, larval stage. Great diving beetles are equally happy on land and in the air, but water is their true element. They spend their whole lives, both as larvae and adults, in and around still or slow-running water and their bodies are superbly equipped for this aquatic lifestyle.

Adult beetles have greenish-black, streamlined bodies with yellow piping around the edges. Like all insects, they have three pairs of jointed legs, and they swim by rowing along with their hairy hind legs, while their middle legs steer. As their name implies, great diving beetles aren't

It may be a water specialist, but this flexible insect takes to the air to spy out new hunting grounds.

Resting on the surface of a newly discovered pond, the beetle replenishes its air supply, ready to go fishing!

just superb swimmers, they're equally at home beneath the pond. They can't breathe underwater, but they don't need to do so. They have their own in-built 'aqualung'! To take in air, they hold their rear end out of the water and draw in oxygen through a tiny opening in their abdomen. Before they dive, they trap additional air beneath their wing case to use as a reserve supply. Once this is exhausted, they return to the surface and repeat the process.

Water tigers

In their own small world, great diving beetles are big trouble. These iridescent bugs may look harmless but they are famously predatory.

Beetles, like many insects, undergo dramatic physical transformations as they grow from immature larvae to adults. In the spring, the females lay their eggs inside the stems of water plants. These hatch into hungry larvae that spend their lives eating and growing. They grow so quickly that they need to shed and replace their skin regularly to accommodate their growing bulk. It's only once they have stored up enough fuel to begin their metamorphosis that they stop eating and bury themselves in the damp mud to pupate. Here, inside this protective pupal cocoon, the beetle develops into its adult form. As adults, they're skilled hunters, able to pursue prey under water with speed and precision. However, their larvae are so fearsome that they're known as 'water tigers'!

With their long, thin body and large, sickle-shaped jaws, diving beetle larvae look little like their adult counterparts. These curious creatures spend much of their time floating

Great diving beetle habitats

with their abdomen at the surface, taking in air, and their head downwards in search of food. Diving beetle larvae are voracious eating machines and will consume anything they can catch. Favourite prey are insects, tadpoles and even other diving beetles, but larvae in their final stage of growth are big enough to catch and eat small fish. They don't have mandibles, so they use their jaws like syringes to impale their prey. Once caught, they inject them with digestive enzymes, that transform their victims' bodies into 'soup'. This gruesome liquid meal can then be sucked up, leaving an empty husk behind.

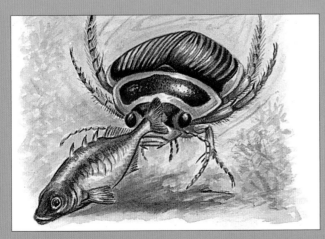

Using sensitive antennae to guide it through the dark waters, our hunter is quickly on the trail of its next meal.

Scissor-like mandibles make fast work of the victim. This stickleback is no match for such an accomplished predator.

Skylark

While most birds go to great lengths to keep themselves hidden from predators, skylarks seem to revel in danger. These little brown birds may look ordinary, but they have far from ordinary habits, engaging in the most astounding aerial acrobatics – regardless of the dangers!

Key Facts	ORDER *Passeriformes* / FAMILY *Alaudidae* GENUS & SPECIES *Alauda arvensis*
Weight	35–42g (1.2–1.5oz)
Length	16–19cm (6.3–7.5in) Wingspan: 33cm (13in)
Sexual maturity	1 year
Breeding season	April–August
Number of eggs	2–6
Incubation period	11–14 days
Breeding interval	Up to 4 broods a year possible
Typical diet	Winter: insects. Summer: seeds
Lifespan	Up to 9 years in the wild

Head
Like many larks, skylarks have a head crest. This isn't always obvious, but can be seen when raised during displays.

Wings
Male skylarks have broader wings than females. This may be an adaptation to help them stay airborne for longer periods.

Feet
Skylarks have three forwards-facing toes and one extra-long hind toe, which is tipped with a straight claw.

Skylark habitats

Ever since the composer Ralph Vaughan Williams (1872–1958) wrote *The Lark Ascending* in 1914, it has been a favourite with British music lovers. Williams wrote the piece while watching troop ships head out across the English Channel at the start of World War I – (1914–18). It's a piece that conjures up everything that the composer thought was quintessentially British and which he worried

was about to vanish with the advent of war. In it, Williams takes his theme from the acrobatic and awe-inspiring sight of the male skylarks' mating display, which is still a popular sight in the British countryside to this day.

When they are on the ground, bird-watchers often refer to skylarks as SBJs, or 'small brown jobs' – a label used to refer to the large number of hard-to-identify little, brown birds that exist. It's in the air that these SBJs transform into one of nature's wonders.

Most birds go to great lengths to keep themselves hidden from predators, but during the mating season skylarks seems to revel in danger as they wheel upwards through the air, singing as they ascend. The verb 'to skylark', meaning to act in a foolish or mischievous way, is said to come from way that these birds seem to risk life and limb with such a seemingly frivolous display. In reality, though, these acrobatics have a very serious purpose. Most male birds sing in order to attract a mate or to defend their territory and the skylarks do the same. And the song-flights they use to advertise their presence and availability to nearby females is truly spectacular.

Dancing with death

The skylarks' performance begins with rapid wing beats as they ascend, almost vertically into the air. After hovering for several minutes, while they sing their characteristically melodic song, they then wheel back down to earth. Such

Comparisons

Shore larks (*Eremophila alpestris*) make their homes in some of the bleakest locations, flourishing and thriving amongst Arctic tundra and bleak, high mountains. Unlike their lark relations, in the breeding season,

the males sprout a pair of black feathers just above and behind their eyes. The aim of these 'horns' is to make them look bigger and more aggressive to rivals and help attract mates.

Shore lark   Skylark

amazing feats typically last a few minutes, but these epic song-flights may be repeated for up to one hour, with birds reaching heights of over 300m (almost 1000ft) before they descend. Often, their calls can be clearly heard, while the birds themselves are little more than specks in the sky.

What's even more remarkable about the skylarks' energetic display is that they also sing when they're being pursued by prey! One of the species' main predators is the merlin *(Falcon columbarius)*, a small falcon that is famous for its own aerial prowess. Most birds dart for cover when predators appear, especially one as determined as the merlin. Not the skylark. When pursued by merlin, skylarks will often adopt the same song-flight pattern, rapidly ascending in circles to gain and maintain height above the pursuing falcon. And, as they soar ever higher, they begin to sing! It's a demonstration of pure bravado. The strength and vitality of the song is believed to be a signal to the merlin that his prey is too fit and agile to be caught.

It's a feat which is so impressive that it has been celebrated not just by musicians but also by poets such as Percy Bysshe Shelley (1792–1822), who hailed the bird as a 'blithe spirit' and John George Meredith (1828–1909), who asked, 'See's thou a Skylark whose glistening winglets ascending, Quiver like pulses beneath the melodious dawn?'. It seems very fitting, then, that the collective noun for a group of skylarks is an exaltation.

Skylarks are a ground-nesting species and have suffered over the last few decades because of changes in farming practices.

Ideal crops are 20–50cm (7.9–19.7in) long and, once a good site is found, males start looking to mate.

Breeding begins in the spring and their choice of nesting site is influenced by the type of crop being grown.

Tracing an undulating pattering in the sky, the hopeful male begins his unique song-flight in the hope of finding a partner.

Wels Catfish

Fishermen have been telling tall tales about these big fish for centuries, but there are some truths in the stories told about these aggressive and active predators. Scaleless, eel-like and equipped with super-sensitive feelers, wels catfish may not be rare or record-breaking but they're certainly strange.

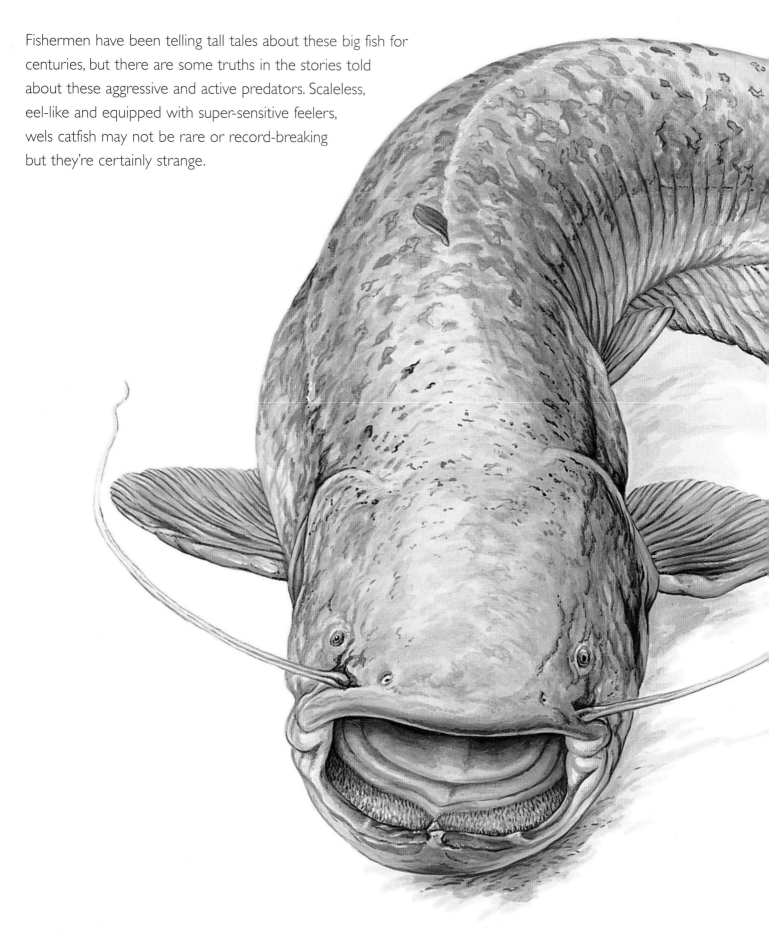

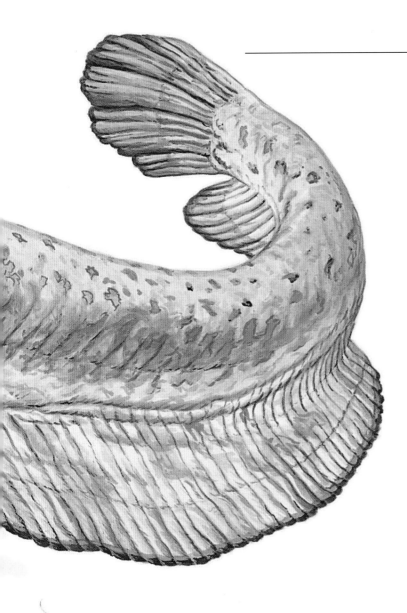

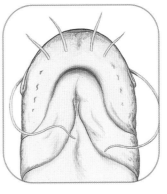

Barbels

These curious-looking 'whiskers' are highly receptive sensory organs, known as barbels, which help the catfish to hunt down prey.

Fins

A massive, elongated anal fin stretches almost to the fishes' tail. In comparison, the dorsal fin (shown) is miniscule.

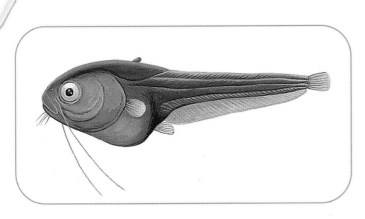

Fry

During the first few weeks of their lives, the tiny, immature wels catfish look more like tadpoles than fish.

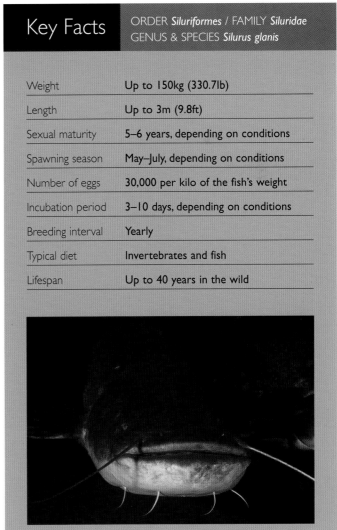

Key Facts	ORDER *Siluriformes* / FAMILY *Siluridae* GENUS & SPECIES *Silurus glanis*
Weight	Up to 150kg (330.7lb)
Length	Up to 3m (9.8ft)
Sexual maturity	5–6 years, depending on conditions
Spawning season	May–July, depending on conditions
Number of eggs	30,000 per kilo of the fish's weight
Incubation period	3–10 days, depending on conditions
Breeding interval	Yearly
Typical diet	Invertebrates and fish
Lifespan	Up to 40 years in the wild

Found in fresh and brackish water, warm lakes and deep, fast-flowing rivers, the wels catfish is one of Europe's most recognizable fish species.

Unlike most fish, wels catfish don't have scales. Instead their green-brown bodies are long and slimy, with an elongated anal fin that stretches almost to the tail. The head is large, broad and flattened with a pair of small, dark eyes set to either side. Inside the wide mouth are hundreds of tiny teeth. These are used to hold prey before it is passed on to two sets of crushing pads located at the back of the fishes' throat.

The size of these fish varies from location to location, but they have long been the subject of myth and legend. Reports dating from the 1850s speak of giant catfish up to

5m (16.4ft) long being caught in the Danube and Dniepr river systems. As recently as 2008, attacks in Lake Schlachtensee, near Berlin in Germany, were attributed to one such colossus. There are even reports, dating back to the 1400s, of wels catfish that were man-eaters. These tales are difficult to substantiate and are probably no more than tall tales or misidentifications. Yet, there's no doubt that these fish are aggressive and active predators.

The young fry live on invertebrates. As they grow bigger, they become more ambitious and, while other fish are their main prey, they'll tackle amphibians, small aquatic mammals and waterfowl. In his TV series *Animal World,* the British biologist Jeremy Wade set out to discover if they would tackle a full-grown man. Well, he released one fish,

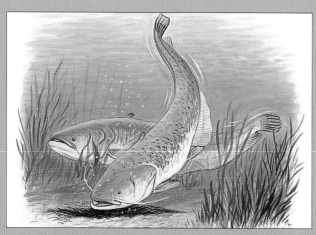
Although solitary by nature, catfish abandon their lonely lives in the spring when they begin to search for a mate.

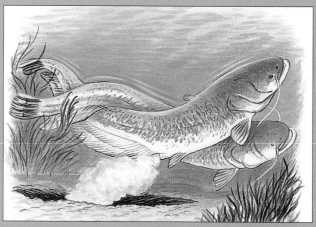
Once paired up, the male digs a nest in the riverbed, using his mouth and belly to excavate the wet sand.

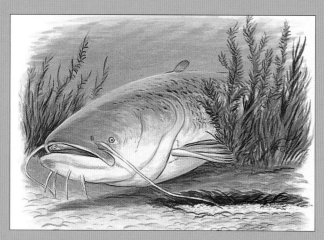
Great clouds of eggs settle in the nest and are fertilized by the male. Now it's just a matter of time.

The father aggressively guards his nest, attacking a passing swan in his zeal to protect the new-born fry.

Comparisons

Wels catfish may have a massively extended anal fin, but eel-tail catfish (*Plotosus lineatus*) have an even more dramatic body shape. As their name suggests, the back end of these torpedo-shaped fish is elongated in an eel-like fashion. Eel-tails are found in coastal regions of the Indian Ocean and western Pacific, from Japan to Australia. Wels are more common in central, southern and eastern European waters.

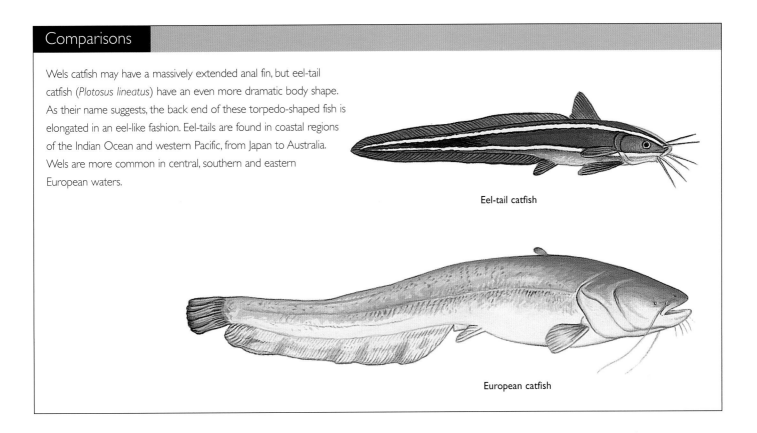

Eel-tail catfish

European catfish

which then circled him and tried to take a bite, so the answer seems to be a definite yes!

Weird 'whiskers'

Lying in wait for prey at the bottom of a foliage-clogged pond would seem to be a poor hunting tactic. but wels catfish have a secret weapon.

Those odd, slender 'whiskers' near the fish's mouth are one of the reasons that this species are known as 'catfish'. The other is that they tend to make a buzzing or croaking sound when caught, which is said to sound like a cat's purr. However, these whiskers aren't like anything that a cat has! They're actually highly receptive sensory organs, known as barbels. Fish that have barbels include catfish, carp, goatfish and sturgeon, as well as some types of shark. It's such a distinctive feature that anglers often refer to this whole group as 'barbel' fish.

These sensitive extensions come in different sizes and are located in different places on different fish. Those at either side of the mouth, which look most like whiskers, are known as maxillary barbels. Nasal barbels extend from the nostrils, while mandibular barbels are located on the chin.

Wels catfish have two long, highly mobile barbels, which protrude from just under the eyes. These are reinforced with cartilage, which is a type of stiff but flexible connective tissue. Two smaller pairs of immobile barbels are positioned under the chin. These weird structures

house the fishes' taste buds and are used to help them search for food in murky waters. They're proficient hunters and, with the help of barbels, rarely miss a tasty treat. When a hungry catfish senses prey nearby, it instantly goes to work. Using the pectoral fins to create a disorienting eddy around the victim, it uses its gaping mouth to suck in prey, which is often swallowed whole.

Wels catfish habitats

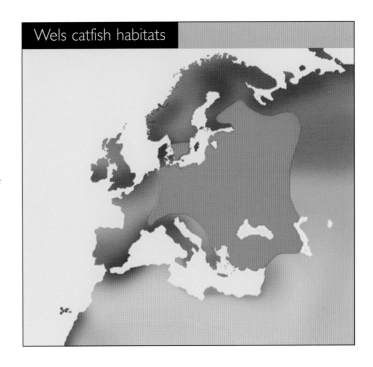

ASIA

SOUTH
CHINA SEA

PACIFIC
OCEAN

ARAFURA
SEA

TIMOR SEA

CORAL
SEA

INDIAN
OCEAN

AUSTRALIA

SOUTH
AUSTRALIAN
BASIN

SOUTHERN
PACIFIC
OCEAN

TASMAN
SEA

SOUTHERN
OCEAN

The Oceans

We live in a watery world. Approximately 71 per cent of our planet's surface is covered by ocean. This immense body of water is usually divided into the liquid equivalent of continents – the Pacific, the Atlantic, the Indian and the Arctic Oceans.

~

The largest of these is known as the Pacific and it covers a colossal third of our planet's surface. Next comes the Atlantic, the so-called 'big pond', which divides the Old World of Europe from the New World of the Americas. The Indian Ocean, known as Ratnakara ('the creator of pearls') in ancient Sanskrit, comes next in terms of size. The smallest, shallowest and coldest of these bodies of water is the Arctic – which is often considered to be a sea rather than a true ocean.

In reality, of course, such divisions mean very little. These great 'wet continents' are all part of one gigantic body of water, which stretches from Pole to Pole and coast to coast.

We all know that the oceans are saltwater, but just how salty it is varies across the globe. Near the equator, the regular rainfall lowers the salt levels. Similarly, freshwater rivers and streams flowing into the Arctic make it the least salty of all five oceans.

Within this great, global ocean, which also varies in temperature across the globe, different forms of life have found their own solutions to the problems of survival, many of which are strikingly familiar. If we were to peer, down, into the warm waters of the Indian Ocean, we'd find 'flocks' of dazzlingly coloured fish, flitting from reef to reef, like tropical birds in some, vast, sunken rainforest. By contrast, a glance into the depths of the cool, grey Atlantic, would reveal 'herds' of aquatic herbivores, being stalked by the ocean equivalents of lions, tigers and bears. Yet, within this rich and mostly unexplored world, life also comes in many strange and startling shapes.

Anglerfish

The name anglerfish is a reference to this species' unusual method of catching prey. These strange, flattened fish have a bony spine between their eyes, tipped with a fleshy lure. This acts like a flexible 'rod', which they use to literally fish for their food!

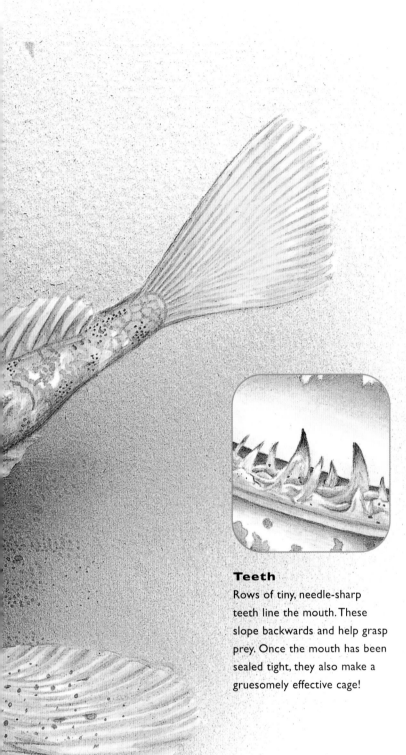

Lure

It may not look very appealing to us, but to a hungry fish searching the seabed in search of food, the anglerfish's fleshy lure looks like a temptingly tasty treat.

Teeth

Rows of tiny, needle-sharp teeth line the mouth. These slope backwards and help grasp prey. Once the mouth has been sealed tight, they also make a gruesomely effective cage!

Key Facts	ORDER *Lophiformes* / FAMILY *Lophidae* / GENUS & SPECIES *Lophius piscatorius*
Weight	Up to 40kg (88.2lb)
Length	Males: Up to 1m (3.3ft) Females: Up to 2m (6.6ft)
Sexual maturity	Males: at over 50cm (19.7in) Females: at over 70cm (27.5in)
Spawning season	Spring–summer
Number of eggs	Thousands
Incubation period	Not recorded
Breeding interval	Yearly
Typical diet	Fish, crustaceans and seabirds
Lifespan	Not recorded

Anglerfish are often described as one of the ocean's ugliest fish! Although these flat-bodied beasts certainly wouldn't win any beauty pageants, such a label is perhaps a little unfair. These fish may look grotesque but they are beautifully adapted for hunting in the ocean's dark depths.

Anglers belong to an extremely widespread and varied group (order *Lophiformes*), which can be divided into 18 families and more than 300 species. Most are identifiable by their flat bodies, huge gaping mouths and fake lures. Indeed, their common name – anglerfish – is a reference to their unusual method of catching prey. Attached to a bony spine between their eyes is a flexible 'rod', tipped with a fleshy lure. Called the esca, this is used to fish for food, and is really part of an elongated dorsal fin. *Lophius piscatorius* has a number of separate, elongated fins, but it's the first of these, terminating in a fleshy lobe, that other fish find so tempting. When prey approaches and tries to eat this fake bait, the anglers simply open their mouths and suck them in, wriggling and whole! Prey doesn't even have to bite the lure; just brushing past is enough to trigger an automatic reaction which flings the anglers' gaping maw open. Lines of backwards-facing teeth prevent any victims from escaping!

More than 2000 years ago, the Greek philosopher, Aristotle (384–322BCE) described a 'fishing frog' which, he said, lay in wait for prey on the sea bed, and used filaments on its head to lure prey into their massive mouths. Such tales were dismissed as fantasy. In 1925, however, it was discovered that anglerfish not only

Anglerfish habitats

existed but were far stranger than those ancient tales led us to believe.

Patient predators

Anglerfish can be found in both the deep oceans and along shallow coastal regions in all tropical and temperate environments. Of the 25 known species of *Lophius*, *Lophius*

Comparisons

The powerful, streamlined body of the Atlantic cod (*Gadus morhua*) couldn't be more different from that of the anglerfish. Although they share a similar range, the anglers' flattened shape is suitable for ambush rather than pursuing prey. Ironically, 'monkfish' (which is what anglers are called in the United Kingdom) were once widely promoted as an environmentally friendly alternative to cod. Now, both species are suffering from over-fishing.

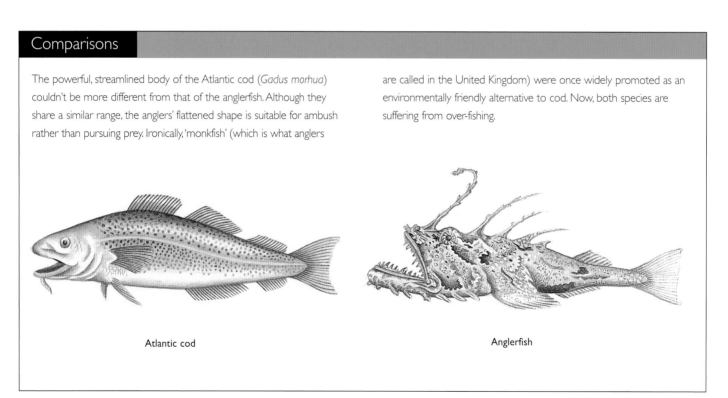

Atlantic cod

Anglerfish

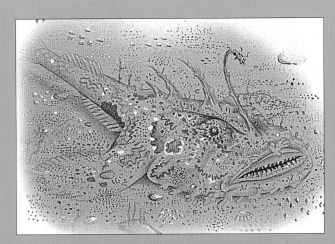

Lying motionless and almost invisible, this predator has learnt that camouflage can be just as useful as speed and power.

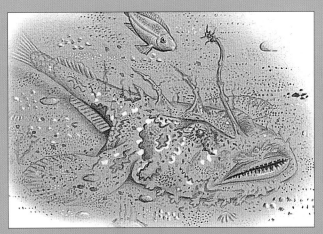

The hungry angler simply lies in wait for prey to pass by, using his lure to attract their interest.

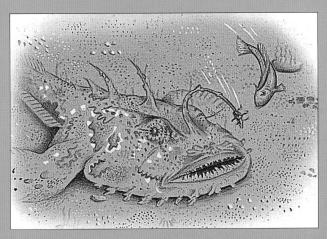

It's a winning technique. As this small fish moves closer, he has no idea that danger lurks just beneath the sand.

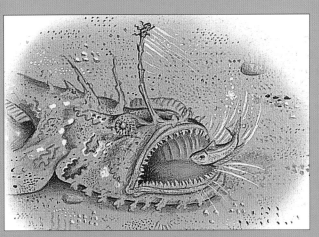

Too late! The vast, gaping mouth of the anglerfish is already sucking in its unsuspecting victim.

piscatorius is one of the most widely known. These voracious predators are found in the central and north-eastern Atlantic as well as the Mediterranean Sea. They live mainly in sub-littoral waters – from the high-water mark to areas of permanently submerged shoreline. Typically they are found at depths of between 2m and 500m (6.6–1640ft), although they often move into deeper waters during the spawning season.

While many fish spend their lives endlessly on the prowl for prey, anglerfish have a more casual approach to catching food. They settle on the sea bed, using their fins to flick sand and bits of debris over their bodies. A border of fringed lobes, which look like bits of seaweed, surround their head and body, helping them to blend in with their surroundings. It doesn't matter if they have a long wait because such a sedentary life means they need very little food to fuel their bodies. They're not fussy eaters, either. Small fish are their usual prey, but one angler was found dead, having choked on a seagull, so presumably they'll tackle almost anything that passes their way!

Being so well camouflaged means that these fabulously odd fish have little to fear from predators – apart from man. They've been eaten in the Mediterranean for centuries and are popular in British fish and chip shops, although often only the fleshy tail (known as 'poor man's lobster') is consumed. Confusingly, in Britain, these large-mouthed predators are usually called monkfish. Other sources call them common goosefish, frog-fish or sea-devils.

Bottlenose Dolphin

Bottlenose dolphins spend their whole lives in the water, but they aren't fish, they're air-breathing mammals. As if that wasn't strange enough, these agile and acrobatic creatures are highly intelligent tool-users with a very sophisticated, if odd, method of navigating around the ocean depths.

Key Facts	ORDER *Cetacea* / FAMILY *Delphinidae* / GENUS & SPECIES *Tursiops truncatus*
Weight	Up to 650kg (1,433lb)
Length	Up to 4m (13.1ft)
Sexual maturity	Males: 10 years. Females: 5–10 years
Breeding season	All year
Number of young	1
Gestation period	1 year
Breeding interval	Average: 2–3 years
Typical diet	Fish and crustaceans
Lifespan	Up to 40 years in the wild

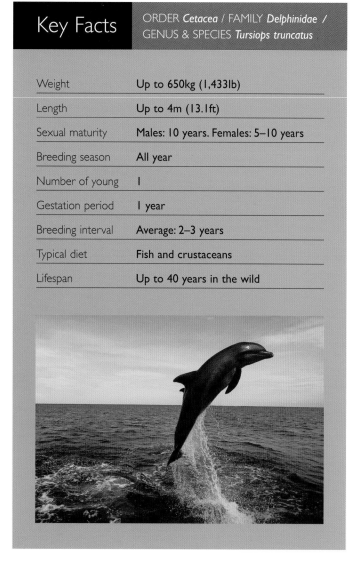

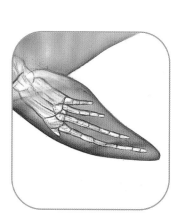

Flippers

Dolphins' front limbs are really elongated hands which, over time, have evolved into flippers to aid an aquatic lifestyle.

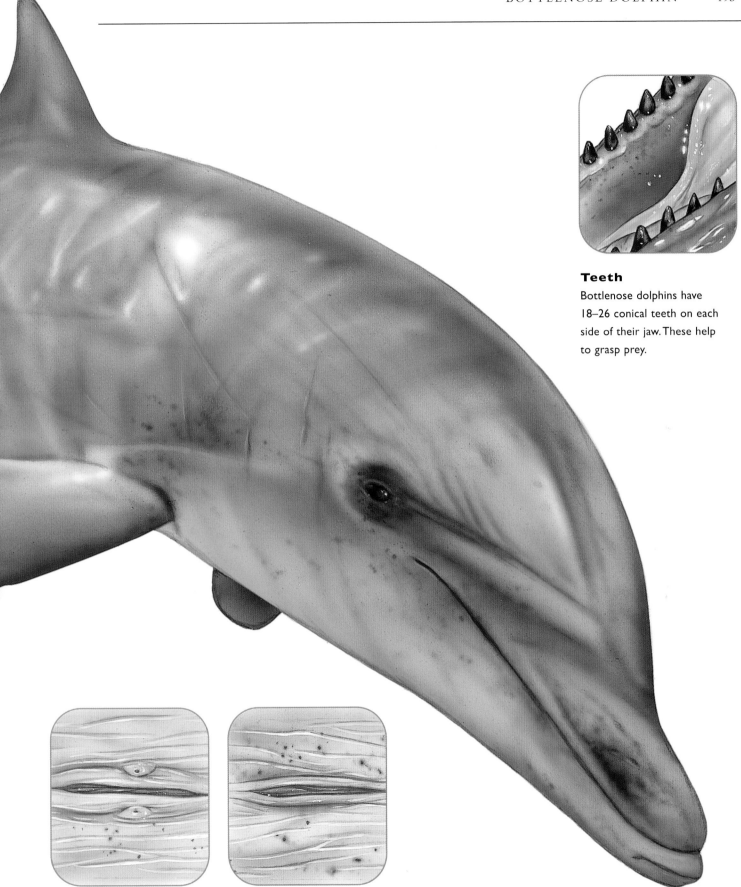

Teeth

Bottlenose dolphins have 18–26 conical teeth on each side of their jaw. These help to grasp prey.

Genital slits

Sexual organs are hidden within slits. Females have one large slit (top left), plus two small mammary slits. Males have one slit (top right).

It takes around a year for a dolphin calf to full develop. However, being born underwater can be a traumatic experience.

Emerging in a cloud of blood, the baby, just 1m (3.3ft) long, needs all of its mother's care and attention to survive.

The female quickly nudges her disorientated calf towards the surface, where he will finally be able to take his first breath.

Now he's free to feed. He attaches himself to his mother's nipple, and gulps down the nutritious milk she provides.

In the water, bottlenose dolphins are creatures of remarkable grace and power. Their large, muscular bodies are streamlined to reduce drag as they swim, enabling them to reach speeds of more than 30km/h (18mph). They're famously acrobatic and can propel themselves out of the water and up to 5.5m (18ft) into the air. When diving, they regularly reach depths of 46m (150ft) – and may even go down as deep as 547m (1794.6ft) when trained to do so. Their characteristic 'smile', playful personalities and intelligence have made them a popular species, and their ability to learn has turned them into animal superstars.

Captive bottlenose dolphins are often seen in aquarium displays and TV documentaries. But these intelligent creatures are at their most impressive when observed in the warm and temperate waters of their natural habitat. Sociable animals, they live in groups called pods, containing between 10 and 20 individuals. Members communicate with the rest of their pod using a elaborate but little understood vocabulary of clicks and squeaks. Unlike humans, dolphins don't have vocal cords, so instead they use sphincter muscles within their blowhole to produce the necessary sounds. Body movements also form part of this complex 'language', which is sophisticated enough to enable them to identify one another and coordinate their activities during hunts. They cooperate with other species too, and will even work with fishermen to help them herd fish into nets, in return for a share.

Dolphins are also one of the few species that are recognized as tool-users. A family of bottlenose dolphins from Australia's Shark Bay famously use sponges to protect their sensitive snouts when foraging for fish on the abrasive sea bed!

Don't forget to breathe!

There are two known species of bottlenose dolphin – the common and the Indo-Pacific (*Tursiops aduncus*). These charismatic cetaceans are air-breathing mammals whose bodies have adapted to a completely aquatic life.

Dolphins are conscious breathers, which means that they have to remember to breathe, unlike humans who do it unconsciously. When they dive, they take a breath using an opening on top of their head, called a blowhole, to suck in air. Once underwater, they have to hold that breath or they'll drown. Thanks to millions of years of evolution, dolphins are efficient breathers and can exchange 80 per cent of the air in their lungs with each breath, compared to humans who can exchange only 17 per cent. This allows them to stay submerged for up to 30 minutes at a time. When they sleep, another incredible adaptation kicks in. It is believed that half of their brain sleeps at a time, so that the other half remains alert to do the breathing!

However, the dolphins' oddest adaptation for an aquatic life is echolocation. Echolocation enables them to hunt even in the depths of the oceans where there is little light, as well as to communicate with each other over vast distances. Bats also use echolocation, and dolphins use similar clicking sounds to build-up a 3D 'picture' of the world around them. These clicks are passed through the dolphins' forehead (called the melon), which is filled with fatty tissue and fluid. This acts like a lens, focusing sounds in different directions. When these sounds hit an object, echoes are received back through the dolphin's lower jaw, and this information is then passed to the brain for processing. It's an extremely efficient – if strange – method of finding your way around.

Bottlenose dolphin habitats

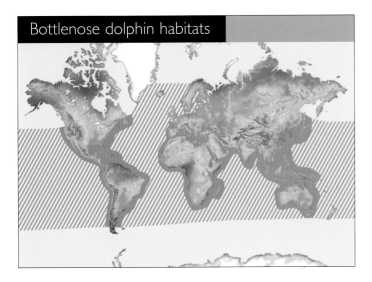

Comparisons

Bottlenose dolphins' powerful, streamlined bodies are 'built' for a life spent cruising through the world's oceans. In contrast, Amazon River dolphins (*Inia geoffrensis*) thrive in silty, slow-flowing water courses. Their bodies are therefore less streamlined, with an elongated beak and a humped ridge along the back rather than the usual dorsal fin. River dolphins are also known as pink dolphins, although they're frequently blue or white.

Amazon river dolphin

Bottlenose dolphin

Cleaner Wrasse

These little fish do a big 'job'. Using their small mouths and super sharp teeth, they're able to pluck parasites from the bodies of other fish. They do this at specialist cleaning stations, where their 'clients' patiently queue for a personal grooming service.

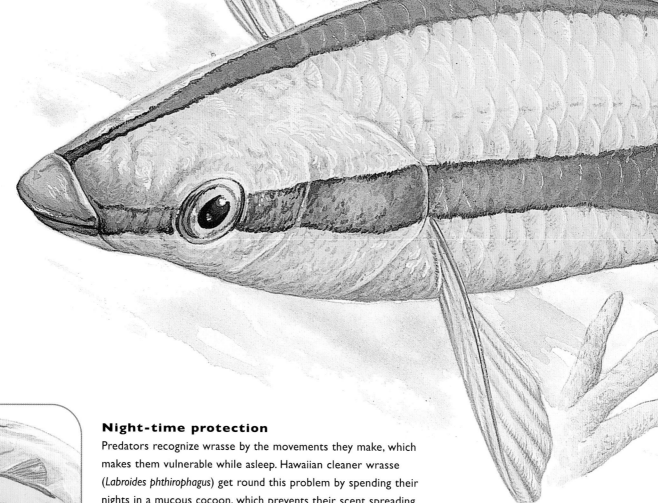

Night-time protection

Predators recognize wrasse by the movements they make, which makes them vulnerable while asleep. Hawaiian cleaner wrasse (*Labroides phthirophagus*) get round this problem by spending their nights in a mucous cocoon, which prevents their scent spreading through the water.

Key Facts

	ORDER *Perciformes* / FAMILY *Labridae* / GENUS & SPECIES *Labroides species*
Weight	Less than 5g (0.2oz), but varies with species
Length	5–10 cm (2–3.9 in), but varies with species
Sexual maturity	Varies with species
Spawning season	June–September but varies with species
Number of eggs	Thousands
Incubation period	Not recorded
Breeding interval	Yearly
Typical diet	Parasites of other fish
Lifespan	3–10 years in the wild

Mouth

A small but flexible mouth enables the wrasse to grip parasites and pull them free from the host's body.

The poet Alfred Lord Tennyson (1809–92) famously said that nature is 'red in tooth and claw', and it does often seem that plants and animals spend their lives in a constant battle for survival. Those that get the most food, water or other vital resources survive. Those that don't, die. So it's surprising to discover that, in the animal world, co-operation can be just as important as competition.

Symbiosis means 'living together' and is commonly used to describe relationships between unrelated species. Commensual symbiosis, for instance, is where one animal (or organism) in a partnership benefits while the other receives no positive or negative impact from the relationship. The cattle egret *(Bubulcus ibis)* is said to enjoy a commensual relationship with cattle, by feeding off the insects they attract. Parasitic symbiosis is an exploitative relationship, where one party usually injures or kills another, such as malaria mosquitos feeding on human blood. Mutualistic symbiosis enables both species to benefit, and it's practised by a diverse cross-section of life, from single-cell organisms to warm-blooded mammals. Some species of ants, for instance, aggressively protect the thorn bushes in which they nest by weeding out competing plants. The Egyptian plover *(Pluvianus aegyptius)* has earned the name 'crocodile bird' because it is said to dive into the mouths of Nile crocodiles to feed on the meat left between the reptiles' teeth. The raven *(Corvus corax)* and wolf *(Canis lupus)* have been seen to help each other to hunt – the ravens call out the location of prey to the wolves, and the two then share the kill. Even humans benefit from mutualistic symbiosis. Between 300 and 1000 different

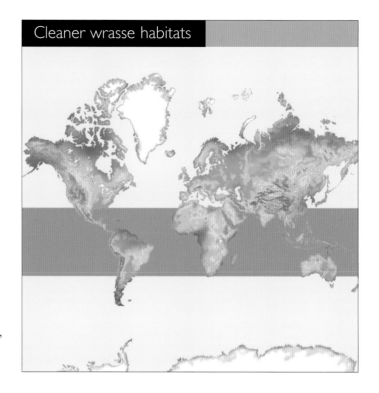

Cleaner wrasse habitats

species of bacteria live in our guts, and these help to keep us healthy.

A specialist service

Cleaner wrasse are best known as a symbiotic species that feed on dead and infected tissue and the parasites that infect other fish. They are famously able to swim into the mouths and gill cavities of predatory species without being

Comparisons

Wrasse belong to the scientific family *Labridae*, which includes about 425 species of brightly coloured fish. Many wrasse are active and aggressive predators and can grow up to 3m (9.8ft) long. Cleaner wrasse tend to be small, torpedo-shaped species, found around coastal waters. They come in a variety of colours but generally have a similar pattern of blue or black stripes along their bodies.

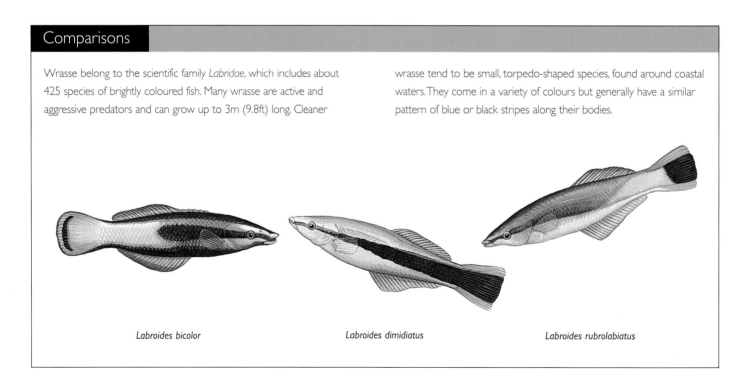

Labroides bicolor   *Labroides dimidiatus*   *Labroides rubrolabiatus*

eaten, because the 'cleaning service' they offer is much more valuable to their customers than a quick snack.

Typically, wrasse operate at 'cleaning stations', although some make 'house calls' if their customers are particularly territorial. Such stations can be found all over the ocean, and wrasse aren't the only species to offer such services – various cleaner shrimp and some species of gobies get in on the act too. However, wrasse are one of the most commonly found cleaners, operating mainly around tropical coral reefs in the Indian and Pacific Oceans.

For a potential prey species like the wrasse to approach a large predatory fish, they have to be certain that they can do so safely, and each cleaning station has developed its own rules. It is believed that fish recognize cleaners by their bold patterns and body movements. So, as the wrasse approach, the fish clearly signal that they want to be cleaned and present no threat. They do this by posing in an 'unnatural' way, typically stiffening their bodies or opening their mouths. The wrasse can then get to work in safety.

Wrasse provide such a successful service that other fish take advantage of their good reputations! The sabre-toothed blenny (*Aspidontus taeniatus*) has adapted to mimic the distinctive dancelike movements of the bluestreak cleaner wrasse (*Labroides dimidiatus*). When fish present themselves for cleaning, the blenny dash in, bite a chunk out of their customer's hide and then rush away before they can be caught!

The services of the cleaner wrasse are highly sought-after, so even big predators must wait their turn in the queue.

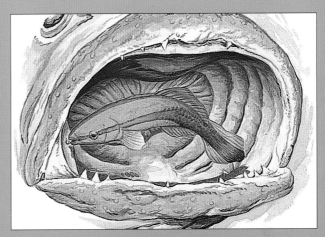

Being small has its advantages. This cleaner wrasse is able to give the grouper a full, inside and outside 'clean'.

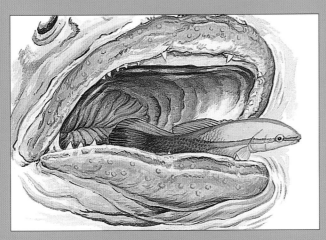

Once he's had enough preening, the grouper will signal that he wants the wrasse to leave by opening and closing his mouth.

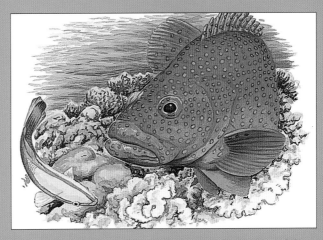

The wrasse doesn't need to be told twice! Flitting out of the grouper's mouth, he quickly moves on to another client.

Common Octopus

With eight arms, no skeleton, a beaklike mouth, blue blood and three hearts, common octopi are truly alien animals. If their appearance isn't strange enough, though, these clever cephalopods have also developed a cunning range of techniques to confound predators and prey alike.

Key Facts	ORDER *Octopoda* / FAMILY *Octopodidae* / GENUS & SPECIES *Octopus vulgaris*	
Weight	Up to 25kg (55.1lb)
Diameter of bell	Up to 25cm (9.8in)
Length of arms	Up to 1.3m (4.3ft)
Sexual maturity	Approximately 1 year
Spawning season	Feb–Oct, but varies with location
Number of eggs	100,000–500,000
Breeding interval	Octopus die after eggs hatch
Typical diet	Crustaceans and carrion
Lifespan	12–18 months in the wild

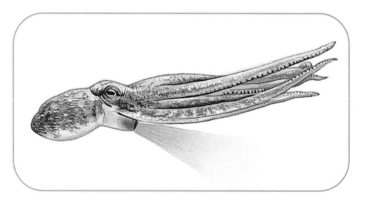

Body
Octopi have soft bodies with no internal skeleton or protective, external shell. They are named after their eight 'arms'.

Hearts
Octopi have three hearts. Two pump blood through each set of gills. The third pumps blood around the body.

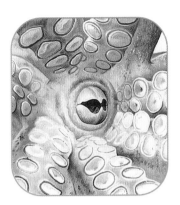

Mouth
Hidden amongst a mass of tentacles is a tough beak and radula (toothlike tongue) for boring through the shells of their prey.

To humans, the ocean can be as challenging and hostile as outer space itself. The area covered by our planets' great global ocean is vast. Much of this is totally unexplored, but even in its upper regions, life is as strange and as alien as anything we might discover on other planets.

Octopi belong to a group of invertebrates known as cephalopods and they are one of the ocean's great oddities. The word cephalopod means 'head-footed', referring to the the way that the arms of the octopus attach directly to its head. Cephalopods, like molluscs, have an exterior shell while cephalods, like cuttlefish, have a small, residual skeleton. By contrast, the bodies of octopi contain neither of these protective structures. Instead their soft, internal organs are defended by a mantle – an extraordinary,

muscular structure that houses their gills, stomach, reproductive organs – and hearts.

Yes, hearts: octopi have three! Humans, like most mammals, have red blood because the protein that binds oxygen (haemoglobin) contains iron. The blood of octopi is blue because their oxygen-binding protein comes from hemocyanin, which is copper-based. This is a poor binder, so to cope with low oxygen levels in their blood, the octopi need three hearts. These help to maintain a constant, high blood pressure.

The octopus' most alien feature, however, is undoubtedly its famous arms. These long, flexible structures are their main way of interacting with their environment and are used for everything from hunting to feeding, mating to

Octopi have short and solitary lives, so when they meet to mate, there is no formal courtship or elaborate display.

Males produce sperm in packages called spermatophores. A special arm (the hectocotylus) deposits these into the female.

Once the female decides conditions are right, she lays her eggs. Now, her sole purpose is to ensure they hatch safely.

The female works tirelessly to clean and aerate her eggs, living just long enough to see her young start lives of their own.

Comparisons

Although cephalopods are usually associated with warm waters, octopi are found in a wide range of ocean habitats. Common octopi are fairly widespread throughout tropical and sub-tropical, coastal waters. Lesser octopi, *Eledone cirrhosa* (also known as the curled octopus), make their homes in the cooler waters around the North Sea and Atlantic Ocean. These curious creatures are smaller than common octopi with red-yellow mantles.

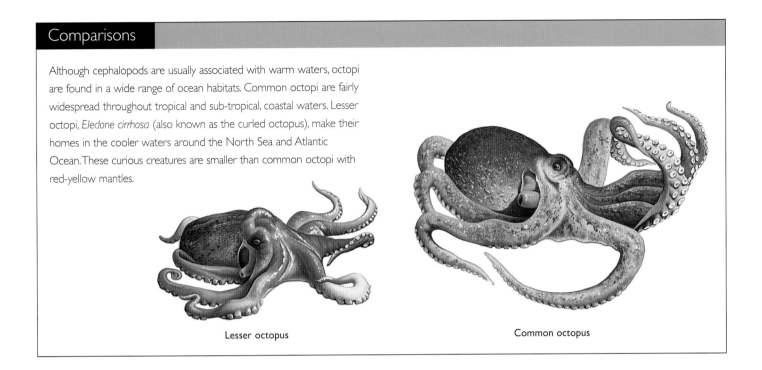

Lesser octopus

Common octopus

'walking'. New studies have even suggested that each arm may have its own independent nervous system, so the brain can delegate separate instructions to each arm, and let them get on with the tasks.

Clever and cunning

Out of the hundreds of thousands of eggs that female octopi lay, few survive to adulthood. Fortunately, fully grown octopi are nowhere near as vulnerable as their tiny offspring. These remarkable beasts spend much of their time 'holed up' in holes. Their soft, flexible bodies allow them to squeeze into and under the tightest spaces where they make their dens. Some species even use discarded bottles and jars! But, if they are caught out in the open by a predator, they have several ingenious methods of getting out of trouble.

Most cephalopods can change their colour to blend with their surroundings. This doesn't just confound pursuers; it also helps them to creep up on prey. A recently discovered species of brown octopus is such a skilled mimic that it not only changes the colour and texture of its skin but also contorts its body to imitate the appearance of specific species. When confronted by a damselfish, for instance, it's been observed to take on the appearance of that fish's enemy, the sea snake. Common octopi are such good camouflage experts that they're usually spotted only because of their habit of piling 'defensive' shells and stones outside their lairs. If camouflage doesn't work, the octopus then resorts to chemical warfare. Its body can pump out clouds of

noxious, black ink, and this temporarily blinds the pursuer and confuses its sense of taste and smell.

But intelligence is the best weapon of the octopus – in defence or attack. The common octopus is one of the most widely studied species and it has been shown to be extremely intelligent. It has a good memory, superb coordination and an ability to learn, solve puzzles and adapt its behaviour to new situations.

Common octopus habitats

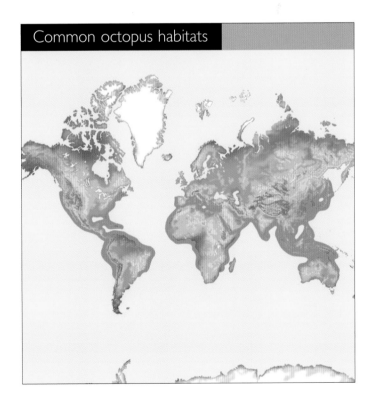

Narwal

With a single, straight tusk projecting from their jaw, no other species of whale looks quite like the narwhal. These 3m (9.8ft) long tusks are so strange that, in the past, unscrupulous traders sold them as horns from the legendary unicorn.

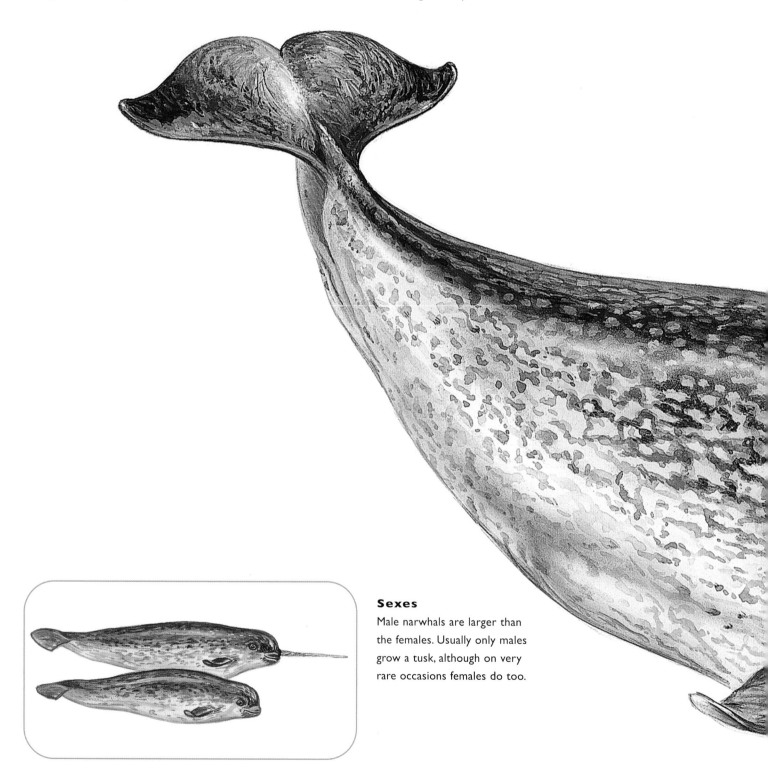

Sexes

Male narwhals are larger than the females. Usually only males grow a tusk, although on very rare occasions females do too.

Blowhole

Narwhals breathe in and out through their blowhole. This is found on top of the head, behind the eyes.

Key Facts

ORDER *Cetacea* / FAMILY *Monodontidae* / GENUS & SPECIES *Monodon monoceros*

Weight	Males: up to 1,600kg (1.4 tons) Females: up to 1,000kg (0.9 tons)
Length	Males: up to 4.7m (15.4ft) Females: up to 4m (13.1ft)
Sexual maturity	Males: 8–9 years. Females: 4–7 years
Breeding season	Mid April
Number of young	1
Gestation period	14–15 months
Breeding interval	3 years
Typical diet	Squid and fish
Lifespan	Up to 50 years in the wild

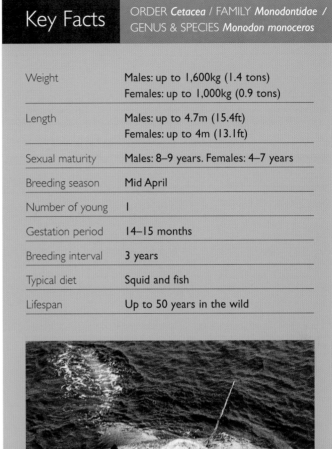

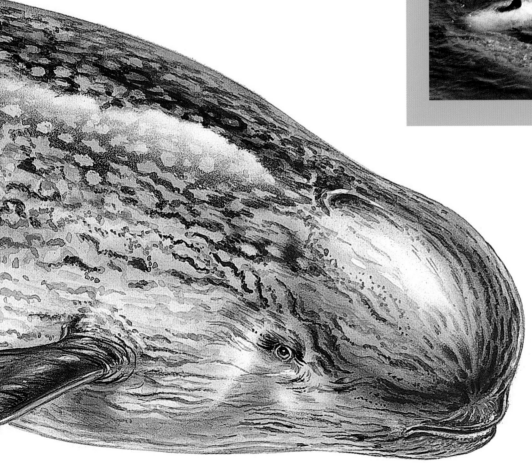

Tusk

This amazing tusk is really an elongated incisor tooth. It grows from the left side of the jaw in an anti-clockwise spiral.

Like all mammals, narwhals hold their breath underwater, and this pod of feeding adults have got themselves into trouble.

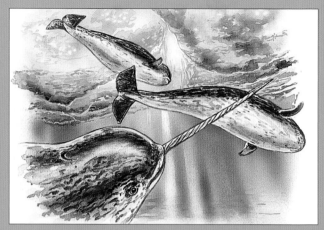

A thick layer of pack ice lies across the water's surface. Luckily, a female spots a brightly lit region, just above.

Narwal habitats

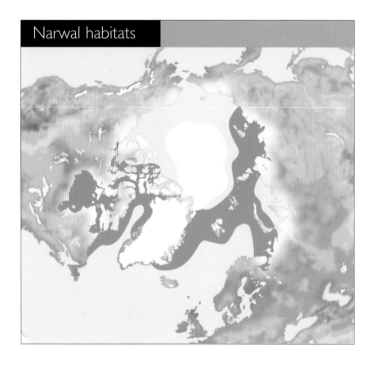

The scientific family *Monodontidae* contains two very unusual species of whale – the narwhal and the beluga (*Delphinapterus leucas*). Both are found in the cold waters around the Arctic Ocean, and in coastal regions in the far north of the Atlantic and Pacific Oceans. They have a similar body shape, with a stocky 'torso', bulbous head and fatty ridge running along the back in place of the usual dorsal fin. They are air-breathing mammals that give birth to live young. They communicate using sounds, and they echolocate, using sound to build up a 3D 'picture' of their environment. However, it's only the narwhals that grow such tremendous tusks.

What's the difference between a horn and a tusk? Horns grow from the head and are made of keratin, surrounding a core of living bone. Tusks are over-sized teeth and, in the case of narwhals, it's one of their two teeth that form the tusk. These amazing appendages grow from the left side of the male's jaw, through the upper lip. One in every 500 narwhals has a right-sided tusk and, very rarely, both incisors develop into tusks.

In the Middle Ages, unscrupulous traders often sold these terrific teeth as the horns of unicorns. These mythical beasts are usually portrayed as white horses with a long, spiral horn growing from the centre of their forehead. Older images show them as more of a hybrid animal, made from bits of various beasts, but they're always powerful and considered to be pure – so pure that a unicorn horn was said to be able to neutralize poison. This made them extremely valuable and one, given to Queen Elizabeth I (1533–1603) of England by the privateer Martin Frobisher (1535–94), was worth 10 times its weight in gold.

Sensitive 'spears'?

Narwhals' strange 'spears' can reach up to 3m (9.8ft) long. That's more than 63 per cent of their entire body length. These amazing structures are the only known example of a helix-formed (spiral) tooth and the only straight tusk found on a living animal. And until very recently no one knew for certain what the purpose of these tusks was.

The ice here is thinner. If she uses her cushioned forehead like a battering ram, she may break through.

Success! The female takes a much-needed breath. By returning to the hole regularly, she'll keep it open for others to use.

The English naturalist Charles Darwin (1809–1882) believed that the narwhals' tusks were a sexually selected characteristic. Darwin is famous for his Theory of Evolution, which he proposed in his 1859 publication *On the Origin of Species.* In it, he notes that many species develop unusual physical characteristics, which have no obvious practical use but which them to attract a mate. Lion's manes and peacock's tails are other examples of 'secondary sexual characteristics'. The ritual of tusking, when male narwhals' rub each other's tusks up, seemed to support this view. Tusking is not a matter of fighting – and narwhals have rarely been seen to fight – but rather it seems to be the method by which males establish rank.

Then, in 2005, Harvard School of Dental Medicine researcher Martin Nweeia made a surprising discovery. Working with Frederick Eichmiller at the National Institute of Standards and Technology and James Mead of the National Museum of Natural History of the Smithsonian Institution, he examined a narwhal tusk through an electron microscope. It was seen to contain millions of nerve endings, which radiated out from the core. This led them to suggest that the tusk is a unique sensory organ, capable of detecting changes in water temperature and pressure. It may also be able to pick up changes in the salinity of the water and particles associated with prey – all of which are vital to the narwhals' survival.

Comparisons

Narwhals share their chilly Arctic waters with a close relative – the beluga whale (*Delphinapterus leucas*). Although both species have a similar shape and grow to a comparable size, belugas are famously snowy white in colour. While narwhals have horns, beluga have their own, equally odd, claim to fame. They have been nicknamed 'sea canaries' on account of the high-pitched squeaks, squeals and whistles that they produce

Narwhal

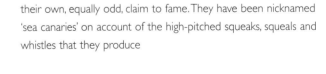

Beluga

Opalescent Squid

In the spawning season, these colourful cephalopods put on a dramatic display by rapidly changing the colour of their skin. Luckily, should this striking spectacle attract unwanted attention from passing predators, they have a few other strange tricks up their sleeves too.

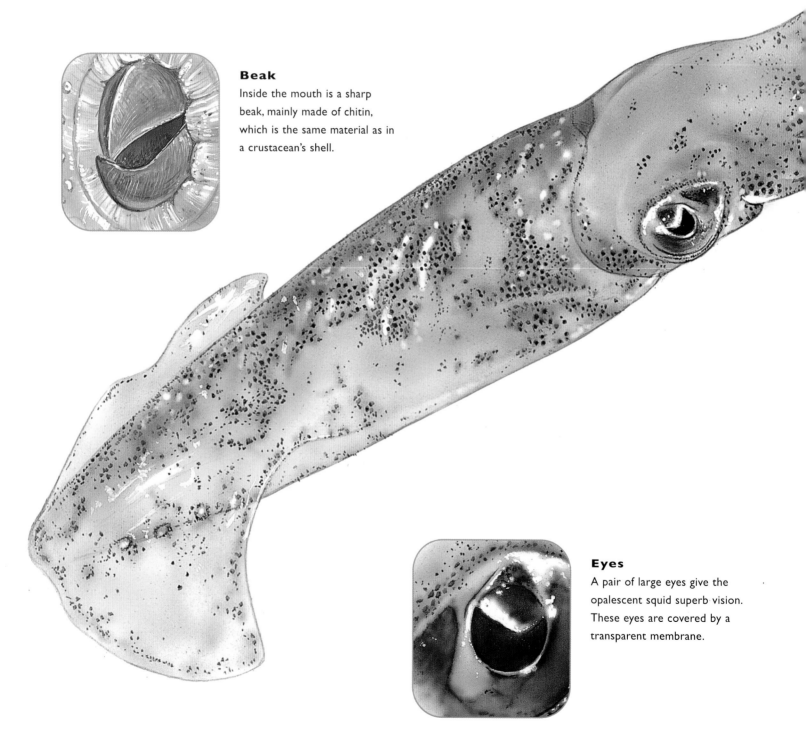

Beak
Inside the mouth is a sharp beak, mainly made of chitin, which is the same material as in a crustacean's shell.

Eyes
A pair of large eyes give the opalescent squid superb vision. These eyes are covered by a transparent membrane.

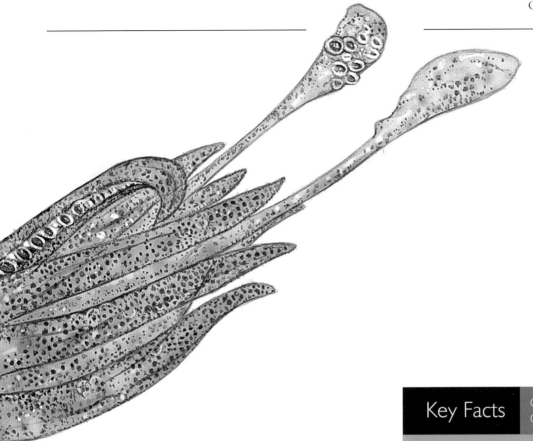

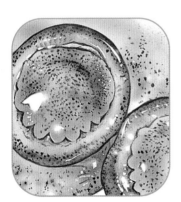

Suckers

Eight powerful arms, arranged in two pairs of four, are lined with suckers. These help grip onto struggling, slippery prey.

Key Facts	ORDER *Decapoda* / FAMILY *Lolaginidae* / GENUS & SPECIES *Loligo opalescens*
Weight	Males: Up to 130g (4.6oz) Females: up to 90g (3.2oz)
Length	Average: 30cm (11.8in)
Sexual maturity	4–8 months, but varies with conditions
Spawning season	Spring
Number of eggs	20–30 sacs, each containing 200–300 eggs
Incubation period	3–5 weeks
Breeding interval	Believed to die after spawning
Typical diet	Fish and crustaceans
Lifespan	4–9 months in the wild, but varies with conditions

Opalescent squid habitats

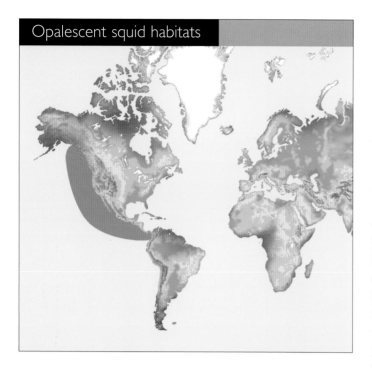

Squid are a type of marine cephalopod. These odd-looking creatures are descended from molluscs, but their bodies are dramatically different. Unlike their ancestors, which had a hard outer shell, squid have soft exteriors. Their bodies are long and tube-shaped, with a small head. The word cephalopod means 'head footed' because, like octopi, squid have eight, strong, flexible arms that are attached directly to the head. These are lined with two rows of suckers and,

in some species, sharp, rasping claws. They also have two longer tentacles, with suckers on the end, which are used to grasp prey and pull it towards the arms. This extra set of tentacles makes them decapods, not octopods. The mouth itself sits in the centre of this writhing mass, and contains a horny beak that is used to break open tough shells. A poison gland lies just inside the jaws, and the poison disables the prey, making it easier to dissect.

These brilliantly colourful creatures reach sexual maturity at 4–8 months, when they collect near the coast to spawn. With a specially adapted arm, males deposit their sperm inside the females' bodies using pre-prepared packages called spermatophores. She then ejects her eggs in jelly-filled sacs. It used to be believed that opalescent squid died immediately after spawning. Death certainly follows very soon afterwards, but adults may survive to repeat the procedure numerous times in the weeks before they die. Once hatched, little is known about how the tiny paralarvae survive, but it's likely they travel to the surface to feed. It takes around two months before they grow big enough to hunt as adults and at least another two before they're ready to breed.

Added extras
Once they're fully grown, opalescent squid are formidable hunters and use a range of adaptations both to catch prey and to avoid becoming prey themselves.

In the wild, the skin of these colourful cephalopods ranges from white to brown, but they can change their

Comparisons

Ever since people took to the seas, they've been telling tales of giant squid. There are around 300 known species, but it's difficult to confirm exactly how big some of them grow because many live in the deep

oceans. The largest known specimen was a colossal squid (*Mesonychoteuthis hamiltoni*) which measured 4.2m (13.8ft). Estimates suggest that they may reach 14m (45.9ft).

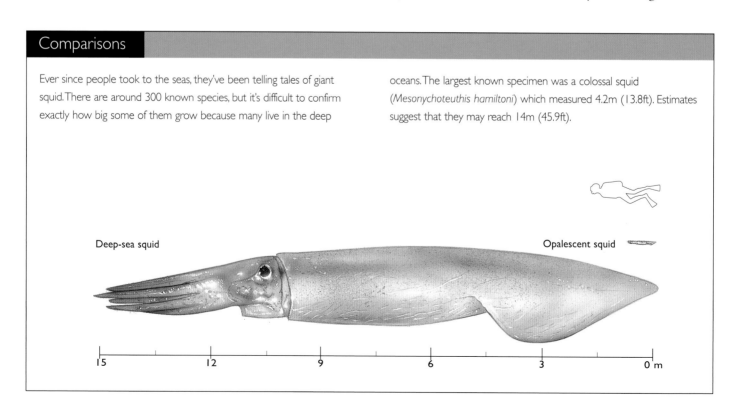

Deep-sea squid

Opalescent squid

| 15 | 12 | 9 | 6 | 3 | 0 m |

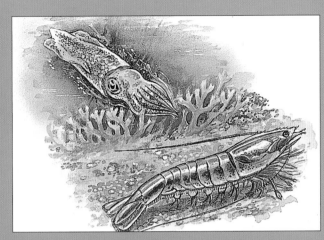

Squid are superb and stealthy hunters, using their huge eyes to help them spot prey in the gloomy waters.

Now the squid's two tentacles come into play. Before their prey can react, it is dragged towards the waiting arms.

Eight pairs of arms swiftly wrap themselves around the struggling shrimp and pull it into the squid's open mouth.

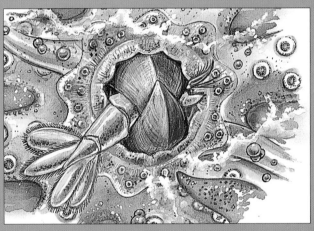

The little shrimp has no chance of escape. The squid's sharp beak will make quick work of its tough outer shell.

colour using pigment-containing cells called chromatophores. This is used to great effect as camouflage and to lure curious prey into their clutches, but it's seen at its most dramatic when squid gather to breed. Then, they put on a striking display, using rapid flashes of colour to communicate their mood and intentions to other members of the group. Interestingly, red is used during both mating and feeding!

However, should this display attract unwanted guests, opalescent squid have a few other tricks they can rely to help them out. They don't have the sort of streamlined, muscular bodies that we associate with the ocean's great speed specialists, like tuna fish, but they don't need to. Instead, they rely on jet power!

The squid's body is enclosed in a muscular sheet called the mantle. If squid need to make a quick getaway, they draw water into their mantle and then rapidly contract it. This forces water out through a 'waste pipe' known as the funnel. Squid can also control the direction of their travel by moving the position of the funnel, which is extremely flexible.

This 'super siphon' can also be used to eject ink. Like most squid, opalescent squid have an ink sac attached to their stomach, which serves as a defence mechanism. Before they jet off, they expel a cloud of dark ink, which temporarily blinds and bewilders pursuers. This dark brown sepia ink was once extracted from squid and cuttlefish and used for ink in fountain pens.

Sea Anemone

Sea anemone are named after a species of plant, but don't let their dazzling colours and innocent appearance fool you. These amazing animals are very efficient predators, equipped with batteries of toxic barbs and a digestive system that can make swift work of the toughest meal.

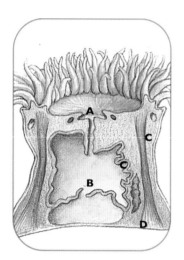

Body

The digestive cavity and sexual organs (D) are contained within the body wall (C). The mouth (A) is the only opening into the animal's inner cavity (B).

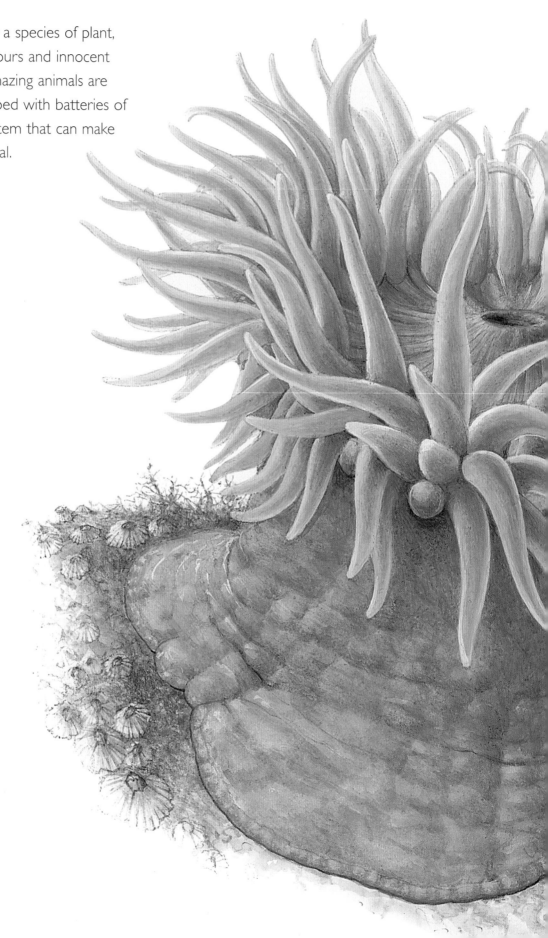

Retraction

When danger threatens, or their bodies are exposed by the receding tide, anemone 'close up', hiding their tentacles inside their body.

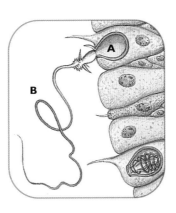

Harpoons

Inside stinging cells called nematocysts (A) are coiled tubes, which act like miniture 'harpoons' to capture passing prey (B).

Key Facts

ORDER *Actiniaria* / FAMILY *Various*

Weight	Varies but most of body mass is water
Length	1.3cm–1.8m (0.5in–5.9ft), depending on species.
Sexual maturity	Not recorded
Spawning season	All year
Number of eggs	Thousands in lifetime
Incubation period	Depends on conditions
Breeding interval	Continuous
Typical diet	Plankton, invertebrates and fish, depending on species
Lifespan	50 years or more

With their bold colours and flower-like shape, it's easy to mistake anemones for bits of marine flora, gently swaying back and forth with the tides. The truth about these amazing aquatic predators, though, is much more strange.

Sea anemones spend most of their time anchored to the sea bottom (or any convenient structure) by an adhesive foot, called a pedal disk. Generally their bodies are colourful columns, tipped by a mass of tentacles. These tentacles are loaded with stinging organs called nematocysts. Inside each of these specialized cells is a coiled, threadlike tube lined with barbed spines. When one of the anemones' tentacles touches prey, the nematocyst is triggered. Water rushes into the capsule, which expels the barbed thread, like a harpoon being shot from a gun. The spine penetrates the prey's skin, injecting it with paralyzing poison. Prey can then be safely pulled into the anemones' mouth, which lies at the centre of the tentacles.

When it's time to breed, anemones use both sexual and asexual reproduction, depending on the species. In sexual reproduction, males release sperm and females release eggs. Once fertilized, the eggs develop into young called planulae, and these eventually settle onto the sea bed to feed, like adult anemones. Asexual reproduction usually involves a portion of the adult breaking away to form what is effectively a 'clone'.

However it has been created, the new anemone can look forwards to a lengthy life. As long as the water remains unpolluted and it is not eaten, an anemone can live for decades. There has been very little research done on this topic but some specimens are at least 50 years old,

Sea anemone habitats

and it has been suggested that sea anemones could theoretically live forever!

Friends and anemones

The world symbiosis means 'living together' and is commonly used to describe complex relationships between unrelated species. Mutualistic symbiosis is where both species benefit by working or living together, and it is practised by a diverse cross-section of life.

Unlike their relatives, the corals, who live in dense colonies, most sea anemone are solitary animals. Yet, within

A harmless-looking cluster of anemone cling to the submerged leg of a jetty, like a clump of colourful seaweed.

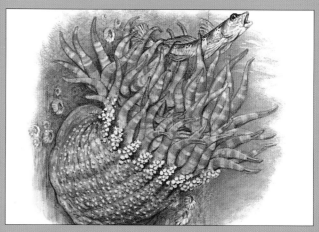

A small fish brushes past, which triggers the anemone's stinging cells. Inside each is a small, but deadly, barbed 'harpoon'.

this large and diverse group, some anemone have found that there are advantages to working with others. Both species of *Isosicyonis,* for instance, live in a symbiotic relationship with hermit crabs. These odd crustaceans have long, soft bodies, which they protect from predators using an empty, salvaged sea shell. Amazingly, *Isosicyonis* attach themselves to the outside of the crabs' shell. This provides the crab with superb defensive armour and makes the anemone more mobile. Sea anemone often spend their entire lives in the same spot, waiting for prey to pass by. They can move if they need to, but it's a slow process. By hitching a lift, *Isosicyonis* can not only feed on the crabs' leftovers but any prey it encounters as the crab wanders.

Clownfishes have such a famous association with anemone that they've become known as anemonefishes. Twenty-seven species in the genus *Amphiprion* and one species of Premmas live within the anemones' toxic tentacles. A combination of the fish's movements and chemicals in the mucus coat that covers their bodies prevents the anemones' stinging cells from attacking them. It's a mutual defence pact. Clownfish gain a deadly ally and they, in turn, prevent the anemone being eaten by butterflyfish. Without the anemone, clownfishes quickly succumb to predators, and it's been suggested that they're so reliant on this relationship they couldn't survive without it.

Comparisons

The order *Actiniariare* contains around 6500 species of anemone. These colourful creatures can be found throughout the oceans but are at their most plentiful in shallow, tropical waters. They vary wildly in size, shape and colour – some are even fluorescent! The beadlet anemone (*Actinia equina*), shown here, is common around British waters while *Isosicyonis alba* is found around the Antarctic, southern Atlantic and southern Chile.

Isosicyonis

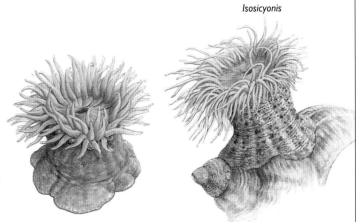

Actinia

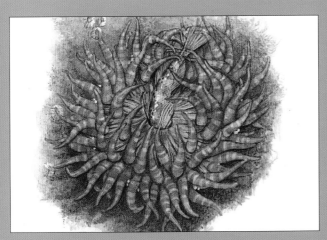

The 'harpoon' injects a poison, which paralyzes the little fish and drags it inexorably towards the anemone's open mouth.

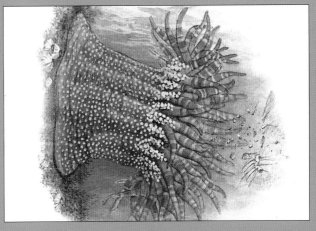

Once digested, the remains of its victim are disposed of via the sea anemone's only orifice – its mouth.

Seahorse

Seahorses get their common name from their resemblance to miniature horses, but that's where the similarity to any land animal ends. These graceful creatures are one of the ocean's most distinctive and easily recognized species of bony fish – and one of the oddest.

Key Facts	ORDER *Gasterosteiformes* / FAMILY *Sygnathidae* / GENUS & SPECIES *genus Hippocampus*
Weight	Up to 226g (8oz), depending on species
Length	4–35 cm (1.6–13.8 in), depending on species
Sexual maturity	Varies with species and conditions
Spawning season	Varies with species and conditions
Number of young	5–1,500, depending on species
Gestation period	2–5 weeks
Breeding interval	Several times a year is possible
Typical diet	Plankton, shrimp and small fish
Lifespan	Up to 4 years in the wild

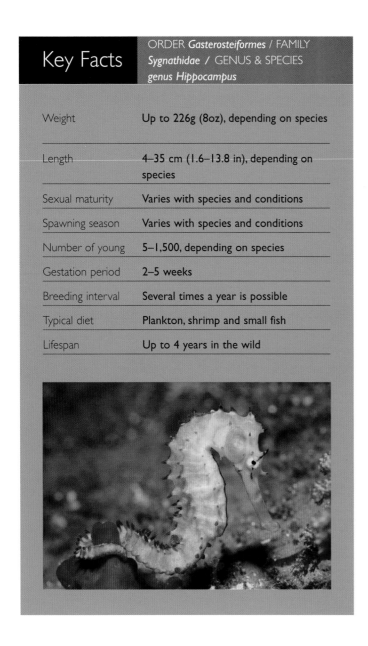

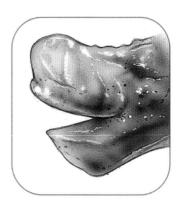

Snout
A long snout is used to probe into cracks and crevices and hoover up any food that's found there.

Brood Pouch

Male seahorses are easy to identify due to the distinctive pouch at the base of the belly. It's here that young seahorses are brooded. They are ejected by muscular contractions once they have developed into miniature versions of the adults.

Seahorse habitats

These graceful marine 'horses' are one of the most distinctive and easily recognized species of fish. They're also one of the oddest.

Seahorses get their common name because they look like miniature horses, but that's where any resemblance ends. These beautiful animals are bony fish, with a backbone, though no scales. Instead, their thin skin is stretched over bony plates, which are positioned throughout the body. Unlike most fish, they swim upright, using a small dorsal fin, like a stabilizer, to keep them vertical as well as to propel them forwards. In most fish, dorsal fins are made of thin tissue supported by rods of cartilage, but the seahorses' fin is an extension of its backbone. Pectoral fins behind the eyes help them to steer. This odd 'design' means that seahorses are poor swimmers and are often found amongst clumps of sea grass or coral, with their prehensile tail wrapped around foliage to keep them stationary.

Their eyes are positioned on either side of the head and can be swivelled in the socket, like a chameleon's (see pages 26–29). This gives seahorses a wide field of vision and helps them to look out for predators and prey. Although they're small, their bony skin offers some protection from danger, as does their natural camouflage. Most seahorses come in 'sea shades' – browns, greens and yellows, which easily blend in with the marine environment. They are able to change their skin colour, too, but are just as likely to do this in social situations as to protect themselves from danger.

The seahorses' oddest physical characteristic, though, is also their most famous. It is the males, not the females, who give birth. The reason for this is uncertain, but it's possible that it enables more matings to take place.

Pairing up
The sight of a pair of courting seahorses is one of the ocean's most moving spectacles.

Comparisons

Hippocampus hippocampus (the common seahorse) is the basic seahorse 'model', but these handsome creatures come in all sorts of weird and wonderful 'designs'. Striking colours, strange spines, crests and manes all help keep these tiny water 'horses' hidden from danger, but the leafy sea dragon (*Phycodurus eques*) is undoubtedly the master of cryptic camouflage. Its bizarre leafy growths keep it safely hidden amongst the seaweed.

Common seahorse,
Hippocampus hippocampus

Maned seahorse,
H. ramulosus

Golden seahorse,
H. kuda

Leafy sea-dragon,
Phycodorus eques

Seahorses can breed at any time of the year, especially in warmer, tropical seas, but in the cooler north they tend to be restricted to spring and summer. It's then that these little lotharios start to look for love, and a couple that are interested in each other quickly make the fact known.

Once seahorses have paired up, they spend much of their time with their tails entwined, promenading and dancing, often changing colour as they swim, side by side. All this bonding has a serious side. Seahorses may breed many times during the season and they need to be certain of their partner's fidelity and staying power. Eventually, when both parties are satisfied, a full-blown courtship display ensues. During this, the male pumps water into his brood pouch, to push it open, as if to reassure his mate that he isn't carrying the eggs of any other female inside. This elaborate 'courtship' can last up to eight hours and culminates with the female inserting her ovipositor (egg-laying tube) into the male's gaping pouch. The male then releases his sperm. The fertilized eggs embed themselves in the pouch wall, where they are cared for until they are fully developed.

Birth begins with a series of muscular contractions that eject the tiny seahorses into the water – and beyond. Now they're on their own, and the male prepares himself to mate again by flushing out his pouch with cleansing sea water. This remarkable process may be repeated up to six times during the year, and the male will almost always return to the same female.

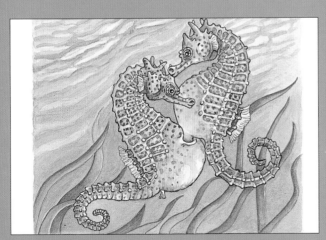

This female seahorse's body is loaded with eggs, which attracts the attention of a determined male.

Entwining their tails, the two begin an elaborate courtship dance, bobbing together through the water, cheek to cheek.

Impressed by his dancing prowess, the female lays her eggs in the male's brood pouch and he releases his sperm.

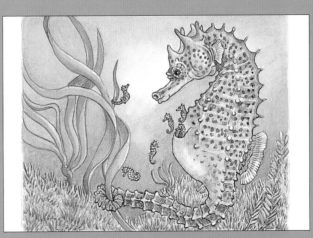

Depending on the temperature, it can take one month for the father to give birth to dozens of tiny babies.

Index